ENGAGE
THE CREATIVE ARTS

ALSO BY SHARON ADELMAN REYES

*Diary of a Bilingual School:
How a Constructivist Curriculum, a Multicultural Perspective, and a
Commitment to Dual Immersion Education Combined to Foster Fluent
Bilingualism in Spanish- and English-Speaking Children
(with James Crawford)*

*Teaching in Two Languages:
A Guide for K–12 Bilingual Educators
(with Tatyana Kleyn)*

*Constructivist Strategies for
Teaching English Language Learners
(with Trina Lynn Vallone)*

ENGAGE
The Creative Arts

A Framework for Sheltering and Scaffolding Instruction for English Language Learners

BY
SHARON ADELMAN REYES

DiversityLearningK12

PORTLAND, OREGON

Copyright © 2013 by DiversityLearningK12 LLC

All Rights Reserved

No part of this book may be reproduced or transmitted in any form, electronic or mechanical—including photocopying, recording, course readers, electronic reserves, posting on the Internet or other online media, or any information storage and retrieval system—without the written permission of the publisher.

For permission to reprint, send email to:
info@diversitylearningk12.com
Or send postal mail to:
DiversityLearningK12
P. O. Box 19790
Portland, OR 97280

ISBN 978-0-9847317-3-2

Library of Congress Control Number: 2013938588

Library of Congress Subject Headings:

1. English language—Study and teaching (Elementary)—United States—Foreign Speakers.
2. English language—Study and teaching (Secondary)—United States—Foreign Speakers.
3. Second language acquisition—Methodology
4. Immersion method (Language teaching).
5. Constructivism (Education).

Cover artwork by Melissa Ketrenos

Book design and typography by James Crawford

Printed in the United States of America

First edition

10 9 8 7 6 5 4 3 2 1

In memory of my mother

Contents

Preface ix

Part I
The Framework 1

Part II
Strategies 17

   Dramatic Arts 19
      Sound Effect Stories 21
      Storytelling with Pantomime 22
      Wordless Books 23
      Puppetry 24
      Sound Sequence Stories 25
      Folktale Dramatizations 26
      Improvisation 28
      Choral Reading 30
      Readers Theater 32
      Greek Chorus 36
      Aromas to Evoke Mood 39

   Creative Writing 41
      Sentence Stems 43
      Acrostic Poems 44
      Process Writing of Stories 45
      Script Writing 46
      Rap 47
      Structured Poetry 52

   Music and Rhythm 55
      Play Party Songs 57
      Infinite-Loop Motif Chants 58
      Teacher-Adapted Songs 60
      Musical Interpretation 61
      World Music Journey 63
      Student-Adapted Songs 64
      Jazz Chants 66

Dance and Movement 69
- Drumbeat Statues 71
- Choreographed Dance Songs 73
- Songs with Pantomime 74
- Storytelling through Movement 76
- Dance Interpretation 77

Visual Arts 79
- Simple Arts and Crafts 81
- Visual Journey 82
- Illustration 84
- Classroom Transformation 85
- Origami 86
- Collage 87
- Digital Photo Essay 88
- Mind Maps 90
- Calligraphy 92
- Self-Portraits 93
- Tape Resist Art 94
- Multimedia Essay 96
- Murals 98
- Book Arts 99

Free Reading 101
- Books, Books, Books! 102

Part III
Sample Units 105

Primary Unit
- Tuesday 107

Intermediate Unit
- The Terrible Warrior 111

Secondary Unit
- Rappaccini's Daughter 119

Part IV
Resources 127

Glossary 133

Acknowledgments 135

Preface

"Here's your curriculum guide," said my new principal. He handed me an austere, official-looking volume.

It was my first day as an ESL teacher in a Chicago public school. I had no formal background to prepare me for this assignment, so I expected the curriculum guide to be helpful. But instead, it only brought back memories of my own school experiences. The pages were full of the same grammar-based language drills that had bored me right out of learning Spanish.

This way of teaching made no sense to me, but I was not sure what alternatives I had. While I tried to do as the principal directed, I was having difficulty staying awake in my own classroom.

Why was I obediently teaching in a way that felt mindless and ineffective? No one other than my ESL students ever came near my classroom, which was located in an isolated alcove on the third floor, far from the "mainstream" students and teachers.

Finally, I tossed out the prescribed instructional activities and designed our own. Instead of memorizing vocabulary for various food items, we made restaurant menus. Rather than learning syntax through drills, we redesigned our classroom, chose roles, and pretended we were in a restaurant. We had a wait staff and hungry customers, and all the students were actively using their second language. Now there were no more sleepy-eyed yawns or heads on desks. The students were awake and so was I.

At home that evening, I wrote messages on index cards. The next morning I distributed them with an air of secrecy. "Don't let anyone else see what's on your card," I warned, tilting my head sideways, widening my eyes, and extending my palm.

X ENGAGE

> *You are in a hurry to leave work. You have a cute boyfriend and he is waiting to take you on a date.*

Brunilda, in her waitress apron, read her card and grinned.

> *You are hungry and tired. You want to relax and enjoy your meal.*

Javier stared intently at his card. He remained silent for a few moments. "Okay," he said "I'm ready."

The rest of the class settled into their chairs, forming a half circle around the improvised restaurant. I turned off the classroom lights, waited a moment, and then flicked them back on. Javier lazily sauntered in and sat down at a table. Within seconds Brunilda was at his side, pointing at items on the menu and pushing him to make quick decisions. As the scene progressed, Javier mimed the process of eating slowly and deliberately, while Brunilda rushed him to finish and be on his way.

"Leave me alone!" Javier finally exploded. The audience laughed. Brunilda tossed her head and rolled her eyes before retreating. I turned off the lights to signal the conclusion of the scene. When we reconvened as a full class, all my students seemed eager to discuss what had just transpired.

This is how I accidently discovered that sheltering, scaffolding, and the creative arts can be a magical combination in second language development. That realization was possible because I disregarded the prescribed methodology and instead allowed myself to focus on natural ways of acquiring language.

Providing comprehensible input — language that the learner can understand — is fundamental to sheltering instruction. Sheltering involves both adjusting teacher talk in the second language to the students' level of proficiency and contextualizing the lesson to assist in their understanding. I gradually learned how to reinforce meaning through gestures, intonation, and facial expressions. Meanwhile, our restaurant scenarios simulated real-life situations that made English comprehensible. Through scaffolding I discovered how to guide students through their lessons one step at a time, learning at levels they could not have reached on their own. Each strategy led to another that was slightly more advanced. My students and I began with the simple activity of constructing a restaurant menu. We ended with a discussion on how motivation shapes human behavior and what happens when conflicting agendas interact.

Grounding class activities in the creative arts stimulated student motivation and engagement. But most foundational to what was going on in my ESL classroom was adherence to an educational philosophy. Behind every lesson was the idea that learning involves more than passively receiving a body of official knowledge. Rather, it is an active process of questioning, experimenting, and discovering — of *making meaning* about the world around us. Some call this "student-centered" pedagogy. A better label is "constructivism." It was my constructivist leanings, not yet consciously realized, that allowed me to create a classroom environment with opportunities for both linguistic and cognitive development.

All of this took place more than 30 years ago. Since that time I have encountered, processed, and revised new information in a multitude of ways, from reading to experiencing. All of this has led me to a conscious understanding of what made my arts-based ESL classes both enjoyable and effective. And it has resulted in the creation of this volume, so different from the official curriculum guide I was given as a beginning ESL teacher!

Part I outlines the book's theoretical foundation, the ENGAGE Framework for sheltering and scaffolding. Part II contains sample strategies that use drama, creative writing, music and rhythm, dance and movement, and visual arts. Part III provides sample units, each one a scaffold that involves multiple strategies. Finally, Part IV lists resources that can help you design your own arts-based curriculum and features a glossary of the terms used in this book.

Engage the Creative Arts is designed for all teachers who work with second language learners, whether in bilingual, ESL, dual immersion, heritage language, or world language classrooms. Yet, unlike most language teaching guides today, it contains no prescriptive activities, vocabulary lists, or grammar exercises. Rather, the book is filled with creative arts strategies that can be revised and adapted according to the interests and needs of your students. It is meant to help you keep your classroom active, relevant, enjoyable — and always awake.

Part I
The Framework

MANY BOOKS FEATURE DETAILED, EXPLICIT STRATEGIES for teaching English language learners. Some of these can be helpful, especially for novice teachers. A major limitation, however, is that they seldom offer a clear rationale for why a strategy works, when it can be adapted to student needs or community contexts, or how teachers can create successful strategies of their own.

This book takes a different approach. Its aim is not to provide step-by-step recipes for instruction. Rather, it is designed to stimulate teachers' imagination, to show how the arts can be used in ways that will engage children while they are acquiring English. More than a list of "best practices," the strategies presented here are grounded in well-researched theories about language and learning. These fundamentals offer a starting point for creative teaching. What's more, this approach can be applied not only to the arts but to any academic content area.

I call it ENGAGE: *A Framework for Sheltering and Scaffolding Language the Natural Way.*

This section traces the development of the ENGAGE Framework from its philosophical roots in constructivism through its methodological base in sheltering and scaffolding, and explores its applications in arts-based education. *(For a graphic representation of the framework, see page 13.)*

Learning Theory

Effective teaching is never a one-way street. It begins with an understanding of how students learn. One important theory of learning — of how humans come to know what we know — has been described as *constructivism*. Based on the work of Piaget, Vygotsky, and other cognitive psychologists, it explains how we build and rebuild concepts to make sense of our surroundings. Constructivism is a key component of the ENGAGE Framework. According to constructivist theory, we learn by absorbing new information, assimilating it into what we already know or believe, applying it to the world around us, and continuing to revise it in light of experience. This is a process that may occur individually or in concert with others. Inevitably we encounter information that makes no sense, that does not fit into our existing conception of the world. Perhaps it confuses us. Perhaps we disagree with it. But it causes us to question what we already know — to push us into what constructivists call *disequilibrium*. It is in this state of cognitive dissonance that possibilities for learning — for constructing new knowledge — exist. While disequilibrium may be uncomfortable at times, it is essential for cognitive growth. Of course, we may misunderstand new information, only partially acknowledge it, or even reject it completely. Yet there is a good chance that we will encounter the disquieting data again, along with another opportunity for cognitive change.

Teachers who grasp constructivist theory, whether explicitly or intuitively, provide environments in which students are active participants. They foster learning through questioning, examining, discovering, and creating. Such teachers view assessment and instruction as interconnected rather than separate activities. They realize that educators as well as students are perpetually interpreting and responding to what goes on in the classroom. They understand that everyone is a learner.

On entering a classroom that is guided by constructivism, you can expect to observe high levels of purposeful activity, hear meaningful dialogue, and see students grappling with new concepts. You might witness lots of movement and encounter lots of noise. Or you might find students involved in quiet but intense investigations, generating their own questions and seeking their own answers. The common denominator is *student engagement*. More specific examples of activities that are consistent with constructivism include the inquiry process in science, problem-solving in math, field trips in science and social studies, process writing in the language arts, and creative arts activities in second language development.

Contrary to a popular misconception, this kind of student-directed learning is a far cry from "anything goes." Teachers play an active and critical role in constructivist classrooms. Not only do they point students in directions likely to be intellectually rewarding. They also use *scaffolding,* various types of support that enable learners to perform at higher levels than they could on their own. This might mean guiding students through a lesson one step at a time, or it might take the form of offering feedback, asking probing questions, or modeling a difficult process. For scaffolding to work successfully, the task must be just beyond the learner's current abilities — not too easy and not too difficult. (Vygotsky refered to this as the "zone of proximal development.") As with a building scaffold, the support is taken away once it is no longer needed.

Comprehensible Input

For students who are learning academic content and acquiring English at the same time, a special, linguistic type of scaffolding is required: *sheltered subject matter instruction.* This methodology was developed in the early 1980s by Stephen Krashen based on his influential theory of second language acquisition, known as the Input Hypothesis. Sheltered instruction is another key component of the ENGAGE Framework.

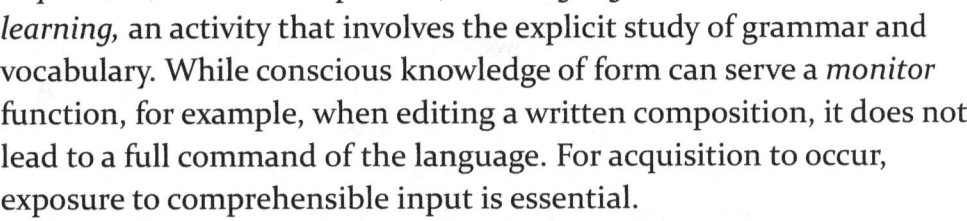

According to Krashen's theory, language is acquired in one simple way: by receiving understandable messages, or *comprehensible input.* Thus a second language is internalized in much the same way as we internalized our first: incidentally, unconsciously, and effortlessly. Krashen draws a distinction between *language acquisition,* this natural process, and *language learning,* an activity that involves the explicit study of grammar and vocabulary. While conscious knowledge of form can serve a *monitor* function, for example, when editing a written composition, it does not lead to a full command of the language. For acquisition to occur, exposure to comprehensible input is essential.

The practical problem for students is that many messages in a second language can be difficult if not impossible to understand. For beginning English learners in a "sink or swim" classroom, most input is experienced as meaningless noise. Intermediate learners may be able to follow parts of a lesson taught in a mainstream classroom, yet misunderstand key points because they lack the more advanced, *academic language* skills.

Here is where sheltering can make a critical difference. Teachers make language understandable by adjusting how they speak and by providing contextual clues. They may modify their speech, for example, through techniques such as pacing, intonation, and facial expression. Or they supplement their speech nonverbally through the use of gestures, visuals, and real-life objects. The key to effective sheltering is to use language for a real communicative purpose rather than to emphasize drills or memorization out of meaningful context. *Comprehension-based* models of English as a second language (ESL) instruction, such as the Natural Approach and Total Physical Response, feature topics of interest to beginning students, along with games and other activities that provide comprehensible input. On reaching intermediate levels, students are ready for sheltered instruction in subjects such as math, science, or social studies.

Paradoxically, sheltering is a language teaching method that does not focus directly on language but rather on academic content that is made comprehensible to the student. So the question arises: What does this mean for the elementary language arts specialist or the secondary English teacher, whose subject matter *is* the second language? One answer is to shelter through the creative arts.

Applying the Creative Arts

Every civilization documented by anthropologists has engaged in artistic pursuits. From the earliest cave drawings to today's multimedia performances, humans have used the creative arts to express themselves and to make sense of their experiences. Besides being universal, the arts have an inherently motivational quality that wise educators frequently tap.

You don't need to be a specialist, however, to participate in arts activities. Painting, drawing, singing, dancing, and storytelling are not only enjoyable; they also provide ways to learn about the world. All too often, schools relegate the arts to mere frills or extracurricular activities, wasting tremendous opportunities for teaching and learning. Perhaps that's because they usually ignore another universal trait of the human species: *paedomorphism,* the retention of certain juvenile characteristics throughout our lifespan. Among the most important of these is play, the learning vehicle of childhood. It is an impulse we never outgrow, even as adults.

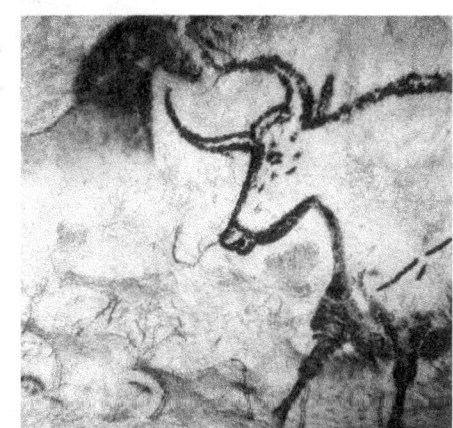

Play is not merely physical, but also social and cognitive, a means of constructing knowledge. The arts take play a step further by channeling our desires to experiment, imagine, and create. As such, they become an ideal way of engaging teachers as well as students.

Bear in mind, however, that there is a crucial difference between professional involvement in the arts and use of the arts in education. The professional arts are geared toward exhibit or performance; thus the *process* of artistic creation matters less than the final *product.* In most K–12 contexts, the opposite should be true. The learning that occurs as a result of active involvement in creative activities — through discovery, inquiry, analysis, and expression — is more important that the quality of a final performance.

When taught in a cooperative, noncompetitive, process-oriented way, the creative arts provide a favorable environment for language acquisition. Obviously, they can offer lots of physical and situational context that makes input more comprehensible. Artistic elements such as music, rhythm, chants, movement, dramatic conflict, and graphic design all contribute in this way. But equally important, participatory arts activities tend to put students at ease, reducing stress and self-consciousness as they try to function in a new language. Krashen calls this "lowering the affective filter" — in other words, reducing psychological barriers that can keep comprehensible input from getting through.

One way to lower the affective filter is through *response activities,* in which the teacher asks students to express reactions to a literary, musical, or visual stimulus, often through nonverbal means. (Oral or written means are also solicited, but the emphasis should be on emotional responses, not academics). Without any forced output, such activities encourage emotional release, intellectual growth, and language acquisition. The example on the next page illustrates how scaffolding can be combined with sheltering in a primary-level classroom.

6 ENGAGE

The teacher begins with a dramatic reading of an excerpt from the poem "Beautiful Snow," by Joseph Warren Watson (1848–1872), sheltering the lines with simple arm movements and dramatic expressions. The students don't need to understand every word — just the general meaning.

Oh! The snow, the beautiful snow,
Filling the sky and the earth below,
Over the housetops, over the street,
Over the heads of people you meet.
Dancing,
    Flirting,
        Skimming along,

Oh, the snow, the beautiful snow,
How the flakes gather and laugh as they go
Whirling about in maddening fun:
Chasing,
    Laughing,
        Hurrying by.

After rereading the excerpt several times in this way, the teacher asks the children how the poem makes them feel. Note that the focus in not on a textual analysis of the poem, but rather on the emotions it evokes. Continuing to focus on student responses, she plays a musical recording that evokes the feeling of falling snow. Then she asks the students to move as snowflakes, using white crepe-paper streamers as they twirl around the room.

With their energy now released, the students are ready to be seated. First, as an entire class, with the teacher modeling and functioning as a scribe, then in small groups, they write a *structured poem* about snow, using the simple form of the *terquain*. Consisting of three lines on a single subject, the terquain offers the opportunity for even a beginning English learner to become a successful poet. For example:

Snowflake
Swirling, dancing
Happy

Next, the children do a *choral reading* of their group's poem to the class. The groups then exchange their poems and do further readings. Finally, the poems are collected and bound into a simply-made book, to be shared with parents or donated to the school library.

Methodologies, Strategies, and Techniques

Consciously or not, all educational *methodologies* flow from and apply a philosophical approach about teaching and learning. In the ENGAGE Framework, that approach is constructivism and the methodologies are sheltering and scaffolding. Sheltering and scaffolding include simple *techniques* — common, everyday practices that become second nature to experienced language teachers. Or they can take the more complex form of *strategies,* which aim toward a specific pedagogical goal and thus require additional reflection, planning, and organization. *(These features of the framework are summarized on pages 14–16 and further elaborated in the Glossary on pages 133–134.)*

A highly structured, prescriptive model of sheltering and scaffolding is not necessary for effectively educating English learners. In fact, mandating any approach that allows for little deviation is likely to be counterproductive. Just as explicit instruction encourages passive learning, step-by-step lesson plans encourage passive teaching. The ENGAGE Framework, by contrast, not only allows for but stimulates creativity. It advises teachers on how to adapt and invent new strategies to meet the needs of their students. So the strategies recommended in this book are meant to activate, not limit, the imagination.

To get started in any new approach, professional development can be beneficial and coaching is often desirable. Teachers need to understand not only *what* they are doing but *why* they are doing it.

Sheltering

The goal of sheltering is to make input comprehensible, by communicating messages — ideally, just beyond students' current level of understanding. Linguists hypothesize that there is a "natural order" of language acquisition. Generally speaking, complex grammatical forms become comprehensible later, and thus are acquired later, than simpler forms. Providing English learners large amounts of comprehensible input enables them to progress to what Krashen calls $i + 1$, the next step in the natural order of language acquisition.

How is this accomplished in the classroom?

- *Focus on content; don't focus on form.*
  Students receive more comprehensible input when their attention is focused on meaningful activities and relevant information than on repetitive drills, flash cards, and similar exercises. Explicit instruction in grammar and vocabulary may produce some benefits, at least in the short term — for example, ability to recall linguistic rules when given time to do so — but it is not sufficient to equip students to use a second language in real-life communicative situations.

- *Don't worry if students make errors in grammar or pronunciation.*
  Making mistakes is a natural part of learning. If sufficiently exposed to comprehensible input, students will acquire correct forms on their own. What's more, error correction is often counterproductive because it makes students anxious and self-conscious, raising their affective filter.

- *Don't worry about output.*
  Students should not be forced to talk. In fact, a "silent period" of up to six months is normal for beginners. Speech production will occur naturally when they are ready to show off their competence. It is the result, not the cause, of language acquisition.

- *Shelter through language use.*
  Techniques include pacing, pausing, gesturing, facial expression, tone, repetition, and redundancy in phrasing. Avoid needless complexity in sentence structure. Do frequent comprehension checks (e.g., through response activities).

- *Shelter through context, hands-on experiences, and visuals.*
  Introduce new vocabulary by building on prior knowledge or using it in familiar situations. Enhance context through manipulatives, realia, games, field trips, and peer support. Make ample use of photos, drawings, charts, calendars, graphic organizers, and appropriate technology.

Scaffolding

The goal of scaffolding in a constructivist framework is to make the curriculum comprehensible while encouraging students to explore, invent, and discover — in short, to help them *construct meaning*. The process requires a knowledgeable adult to support children or adolescents through each new phase of learning. Helping them succeed in small steps builds their confidence and creates momentum to climb higher. The constructivist teacher plans a logical sequence of activities, but avoids guiding students toward one "correct" answer or toward a predetermined skill-set. Her goal is to assist them in thinking independently, critically, and creatively — that is, to foster active rather than passive learning. Thus she keeps activities within the zone of proximal development, providing and removing support as appropriate, while incorporating as much student choice as possible.

How are these principles of scaffolding applied in practice?

- *Structure lessons around classroom rituals and routines.*
  When children are facing unfamiliar situations on a daily basis, knowing what to expect can make lessons more comprehensible and students more willing to take risks. For example, it helps to use a familiar format when introducing new material and to set regular times for science experiments, cooperative group activities, and free voluntary reading.

- *Create opportunities for all students to participate.*
  When English learners are taught in mainstream classrooms, teachers need to perform a careful balancing act. They must work hard to ensure that no student is excluded from an activity because of language difficulties and, at the same time, that no student is bored by oversimplified content. One solution is to make ample use of response activities, as described in many of the strategies in Part II. But there are several others: Give students plenty of choices. Make learning a collective enterprise by choosing problems that can be solved with peer support. Encourage students who have become expert in a subject or skill to assist their peers by using scaffolding techniques that the teacher has modeled.

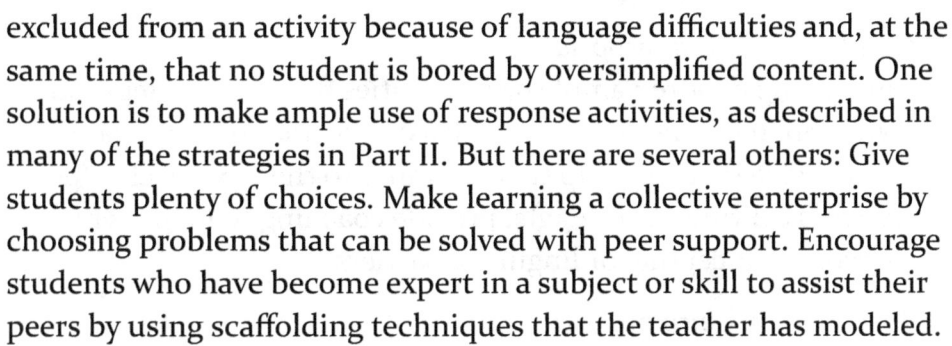

- *Build on what students already know or believe.*
  An important principle of constructivism is that knowledge is never acquired in a vacuum. We take in, evaluate, and organize new information in relation to the ideas we already possess. Often this

process results in conflicts, which in turn become the source of different or deeper insights. To help students take full advantage of such learning opportunities, teachers can assist them in clarifying what they currently know or believe as the foundation for new learning.

- *Stress conceptual understanding.*
  True learning involves cognitive change. It means building and rebuilding mental structures as we interpret the world around us. Thus constructivist teachers recognize the importance of elevating projects and discussions to a conceptual level, encouraging students to reflect and generalize about their experience.

- *Provide expert modeling.*
  By thinking out loud, model your own processes of critical questioning, problem-posing, and conceptual analysis. Demonstrate tasks and coach students who are grappling with especially difficult ones. Bring outside experts into the classroom to demonstrate projects, experiments, and other learning activities.

- *Encourage questioning.*
  Take a skeptical approach toward official knowledge and "expert" opinion, modeling the habits of critical analysis. Ask open-ended questions that lead to new and unexpected lines of inquiry and let students pursue their own answers. Encourage them to pose their own problems. When the opportunity arises, turn those problems into research projects.

- *Give feedback at appropriate times.*
  After giving children ample opportunities to solve problems on their own, step in before they become frustrated and lose motivation. Offer advice that will help them advance to the next level. When students continue to struggle, provide coaching to help them overcome conceptual or linguistic barriers.

- *Turn mistakes into opportunities.*
  Make it clear that mistakes are normal, everyday occurrences — and not just for students but for teachers as well. When analyzed and discussed, they can also provide an important stimulus for learning because they prompt us to rethink our existing ideas.

Classroom Environment

No methodology, however effective, can work wonders on its own. Teaching and learning are among the most complex of human activities, in part because they occur in *contexts* that often matter as much as instruction itself. To make sheltering and scaffolding as effective as possible, here are some guidelines for shaping the classroom environment:

- *Lower the affective filter.*
  An environment that feels safe and secure, in which it's OK to make mistakes, is essential to authentic learning. Arts-based activities, in which there are many "correct" answers, can play an important role here. But any lesson that is compelling and engaging can lower the affective filter by making students forget they are learning in a second language.

- *Incorporate lots of free voluntary reading.*
  Krashen notes that reading is the most effective way to acquire academic language. Studies have also shown that when books are freely chosen by students, their reading tends to be more extensive.

- *Don't hesitate to use students' first language when other techniques are failing to clarify an important point.*
  But be careful not to let your students expect regular translation of words or concepts. Too much "native language support" can encourage them to tune out input in the second language. Language separation is especially important in dual immersion programs.

- *Ensure that resources are available.*
  Besides being equipped with movable furniture and ample space for learners to interact, classrooms should be well supplied with books on subjects of interest to students; maps, charts, and other visuals; computers, software, Internet connections, and multimedia; materials that stimulate artistic activities; and items from the natural world, such as fish tanks, terrariums, and ant colonies. Other key resources include trips to museums, zoos, aquariums, plays, concerts, science fairs, and various community- and family-oriented events.

- *Use authentic assessment.*
  Incorporate informal, ongoing assessments to gauge students' day-to-day progress in a low-stress environment. Focus primarily on their responses and performance in classroom activities, as shown in the *What to Look for* section of each strategy in Part II.

Frameworks in Perspective

No educational framework or model or approach can encompass every aspect of teaching and learning. Those that claim to do so should be viewed with skepticism. In my experience, the best classrooms are too alive, too vibrant, to be restricted by a single overarching structure. Spontaneity should be welcomed, not squelched in the name of preconceived "objectives," rigid lesson plans, or "research based" models. I believe that frameworks are only valuable to the extent they stimulate creativity and discovery in both teachers and students. Their role is simply to provide a conceptual basis for instruction, a purposeful way of using methodologies, strategies, and techniques.

This was my aim in developing the ENGAGE Framework: to create a theoretically grounded approach to sheltering and scaffolding for second language learners. In no way does it exclude the use of other methodologies. In fact, it implies a role for culturally responsive pedagogy and native language instruction, even though they are not key components. The ENGAGE Framework is also compatible with discovery learning, problem-based learning, and other forms of constructivism. On the other hand, it is *not* compatible with transmission models that feature methodologies such as direct, explicit instruction in grammar and vocabulary.

The graphic on the facing page shows the basic elements of the ENGAGE Framework, beginning with a large star representing the constructivist philosophy that guides it. The nearby hexagons depict four important features of the classroom environment. At the bottom of the graphic are ovals that identify sheltering and scaffolding techniques used informally throughout the day. These are incorporated into the strategies at the center of the diagram, a progression of which leads toward a specific curricular goal.

Finally, it's important to reiterate that the ENGAGE Framework can be applied to virtually any type of academic content. My hope is that educators will use it as a guide to teaching language not only through the creative arts — the focus of this volume — but across the curriculum in language arts, math, science, and social studies.

The Engage Framework

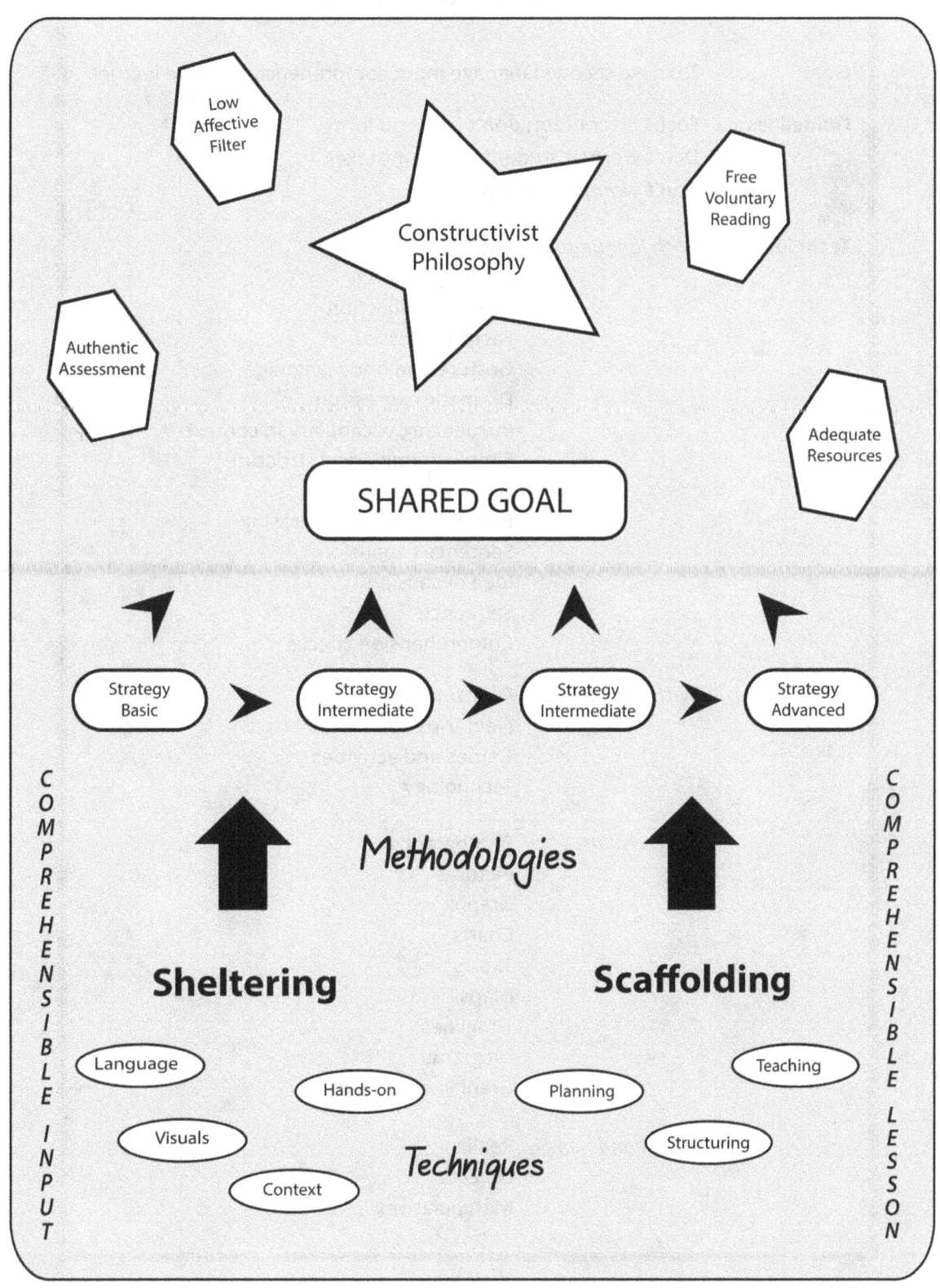

Sheltering Overview

Goal	To make second language input comprehensible to the learner	
Guidelines	Focus on content; don't focus on form	
	Don't worry if students make mistakes	
	Don't worry about output	
Techniques	*With language*	Pacing and pauses
		Clarity of speech
		Tone and inflection
		Facial expression
		Gesture and body language
		Dramatic expression
		Introducing vocabulary in context
		Simple grammatical structure
		Tense control
		Redundancy and rephrasing
		Sentence expansion
		Idea expansion
		Sequence
		Comprehension checks
	With context	Peer support
		Field trips and excursions
		Games and activities
		Technology
	With visuals	Photographs
		Pictures
		Graphs
		Charts
		Tables
		Maps
		Timelines
		Diagrams
		Graphic organizers
	With hands-on	Realia
		Objects
		Manipulatives

Scaffolding Overview

Goals To make curriculum comprehensible to the learner

To create momentum for learning by helping students succeed in small steps

To encourage self-directed learning by providing assistance to students, enabling them to think independently, critically, and creatively

Guidelines Keep activities within the zone of proximal development

Provide and remove support as appropriate

Incorporate as much choice as possible

Techniques *Planning* Beginning with simple tasks to boost students' confidence

Planning a logical sequence of activities

Fostering active rather than passive learning

Focusing on process, not product

Structuring Choosing problems that can be solved with peer support

Using ritual and routine

Enabling all students to participate at their own linguistic and academic level

Incorporating response activities

Teaching Building on prior knowledge

Stressing conceptual understanding

Modeling your own thought process by "thinking out loud"

Demonstrating how to perform tasks

Using expert models

Posing problems, inviting questions

Providing feedback, offering explanations

Coaching learners who continue to struggle

Transforming student mistakes into learning opportunities

Examples of Sheltering and Scaffolding Strategies

Creative Arts
Choral Reading
Jazz Chants
Pantomime
Puppetry
Readers Theater
Structured Poetry

Language Arts
Dialogue Journals
Jigsaw
KWL
Literature Circles
Read Alouds
Response Journals
Think Alouds
Think Pair Share
T-Journals

Social Studies
Fishbowl
Jigsaw
KWL
Mock Trials
Oral Histories
Response Journals
Think Pair Share
Timelines

Mathematics
Board Games
Learning Centers
Response Journals
Student Generated Word Problems
Think Aloud
Think Pair Share

Science
Experiments
Jigsaw
KWL
Learning Centers
Observation Journals
Think Pair Share

Part II
Strategies

THE CREATIVE ARTS NOT ONLY ENRICH the classroom environment. They also provide ideal conditions for language acquisition, fostering high levels of student engagement and motivation along with low levels of stress and self-consciousness. What's more, the creative arts offer countless opportunities for sheltering English and scaffolding academic content.

Strategies for illustrating those opportunities are the subject of this section. They are organized by discipline — Dramatic Arts, Creative Writing, Music and Rhythm, Dance and Movement, and Visual Arts — with cross-listings where a strategy draws on multiple art forms. Each activity is specifically recommended for primary, intermediate, or secondary classrooms, although several can be adapted for any level of the K–12 curriculum. Many can and should be expanded, depending on the goals of the teacher, or tailored to multiple levels of English proficiency.

The strategies are designed to engage students enrolled in a variety of programs, including English as a second language, structured English immersion, transitional bilingual education, developmental bilingual education, dual language immersion, heritage language instruction, and the teaching of world languages. The sheltering techniques are adaptable for use with English learners in either dedicated or mainstream classrooms. And the scaffolding techniques can be helpful for all students, regardless of their language skills.

A common template is used in outlining the strategies *(see next page)*. While instructional *Goals* are included, you will note the absence of "language objectives" and "content objectives." That's because behavioral objectives (i.e., predetermined, testable outcomes) impose constraints on student-directed learning. They imply that anything worth knowing is easily measured, while creating an artificial separation between assessment and instruction. Such concepts have no place in a constructivist framework like ENGAGE. Nor do reinforcement techniques, whether positive or negative. Instead, under *What to Look for*, you will find ideas for informal and authentic assessment.

The template also features *Extensions*, or possibilities for elaborating the strategy within your own classroom, and *Adaptations*, or ideas for using it in other contexts.

> **Strategy Template**
>
> Instructional Level (K–3, 4–6, or 7–12)
> Goal
> Explanation
> Example
> Materials
> Guidelines
> Extensions
> Adaptations
> What to Look for
> Resources

Some strategies are marked as *Response Activities*, in which the teacher invites students to express their reactions to an activity by verbal or nonverbal means.

Art or Science?

These days terms like "research based" and "scientifically validated" are applied widely — and loosely — to instructional models, usually in the absence of rigorous studies. I make no such claim for the strategies recommended here. As noted in Part I, the ENGAGE Framework is based on well-established theories about language and learning. But applying those theories in the classroom is more of an art than a science. There is no simple formula of sheltering and scaffolding that works for every teacher, in every classroom, with every student. In fact, highly prescriptive, "teacher-proof" approaches are likely to fail. Learning is above all a creative, open-ended enterprise, and so is effective teaching. The strategies that follow take that philosophy as their starting point. Where they end up depends on you.

Dramatic Arts

I regard the theatre as the greatest of all art forms, the most immediate way in which a human being can share with another the sense of what it is to be a human being.

Oscar Wilde

DRAMATIC ARTS BRING EMOTIONAL RESPONSE, self-discovery, and social interaction to the classroom. Recognizing ourselves and others through storytelling, oral interpretation, and drama heightens our engagement and causes us to reflect upon who we are and what we do.

The dramatic arts activities in this section facilitate language development through storytelling, oral interpretation, and creative drama. *Storytelling* takes many forms, from the purely anecdotal to the formal written genre. *Oral interpretation* can be as basic as the teacher reading children's or young adult literature aloud, sheltering through dramatic expression as he goes along. But when students do the interpreting in their second language, it can be challenging. Readers Theater and choral reading, on the other hand, provide ways of sheltering language so it can be understood and acquired.

Children's drama is an art form in its own right. Rather than career training, however, its goal is cognitive and affective development. It consists of two genres, children's theater and creative drama. While the former emphasizes *product* (formal productions acted by adults for children or children for children), the latter focuses on *process,* the learning possibilities opened up by engaging students in drama. Creative drama uses informal and engaging techniques such as improvisation. And it taps into our inherent love of play, which in second language contexts has the additional advantage of lowering the affective filter. Drama activities can also segue into creative writing when students produce scripts based on their improvisations. Because of the emphasis on process, creative drama activities are featured in this section, while children's theater activities are not.

Dramatic Arts Strategies*

Primary (K–3)
- Sound Effect Stories 21
- Storytelling with Pantomime 22
- Songs with Pantomime 74

Primary – Intermediate (K–6)
- Wordless Books 23
- Puppetry 24
- Visual Journey 82

Intermediate (4–6)
- Sound Sequence Stories 25
- Folktale Dramatizations 26
- Musical Interpretation 61
- Storytelling through Movement 76

Intermediate – Secondary (4–12)
- Improvisation 28
- Choral Reading 30
- Readers Theater 32
- Script Writing 46

Secondary (7–12)
- Greek Chorus 36
- Dance Interpretation 77

All levels (K–12)
- Aromas to Evoke Mood 39
- Books, Books, Books! 102

*Including cross-listings from Creative Writing, Music and Rhythm, Dance and Movement, Visual Arts, and Free Reading.

DRAMATIC ARTS 21

Sound Effect Stories

Response Activity

Instructional Level
Primary (K–3)

Goal
To provide context for beginning English language acquisition through sound

Explanation
The teacher gives a dramatic reading of a short and interesting story. During a subsequent reading, she invites the students to make sounds to accompany the story, for example, the wind blowing or dogs barking. As a way to manage noise levels, she uses a "volume control wheel." To create this device, pictured below, cut a large half-circle out of cardboard and use a paper fastener to attach an arrow, which can be rotated from Soft to Loud.

Materials
- Story or story book
- Volume control wheel

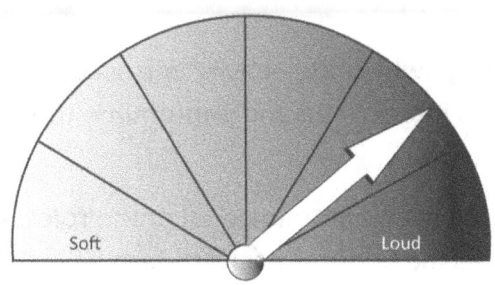

Guideline
The teacher should practice using the volume control wheel with the students before integrating it with the story.

Extension
In a story with a repeated refrain, the volume control wheel may be used with the refrain and the sound effects, or with the refrain alone.

Adaptation
This strategy can be used with oral stories as well. Since visuals are helpful in providing comprehensible input, the teacher may want to use pictures or drawings to help move the story along, displaying them at helpful points during the initial telling.

What to Look for
Students should be providing sound effects at appropriate times during the story.

Storytelling with Pantomime

Response Activity

Instructional Level
Primary (K–3)

Goal
To provide context for beginning English language acquisition through pantomime

Explanation
The teacher gives a dramatic reading of a simple story. During a subsequent reading, he invites students to pantomime various characters while he reads. No roles are assigned; all of the children pantomime all of the characters. Because everyone is active simultaneously, there is no audience; this keeps the affective filter low. Language is sheltered through gesture and movement that clarify and reinforce meaning.

Materials
- Story or picture book

Guideline
Set physical parameters in which the activity will occur. A simple way is to have all the children pull their chairs into a circle and pantomime the story's action within.

Extensions
After all of the students have pantomimed all of the roles, the teacher may ask for volunteers or assign specific roles for each student. Then he rereads the story as the students pantomime their individual parts.

Keep in mind that even inanimate objects such as trees can be portrayed in pantomime. This helps to ensure that all students in the class will be involved in the activity and that there is no audience to make them self-conscious.

Adaptation
This strategy can be used with oral stories as well. Since pictures are helpful in giving comprehensible input, the teacher may consider using pictures or drawings to hold up at helpful points during the initial telling.

What to Look for
Student gesture and movement should be consistent with the story line.

Wordless Books

Response Activity

Instructional Level
Primary – Intermediate (K–6)

Goal
To provide context for English language acquisition through storytelling

Explanation
Wordless books have evocative, sequential pictures with little or no text, created specifically to elicit a response. They can be used to stimulate conversation in the second language or to generate student writing. The creation of a wordless book can be an alternative to a written story for a child in the early stages of English language acquisition.

Materials
- Wordless book or picture book with the text covered
- Post-its

Guidelines
The teacher displays the pictures sequentially to the students and leads a discussion about what is happening on each page, using the images to shelter her words.

Extensions
Divide the students into groups and have each one appoint a scribe. Give them a wordless book (either the one previously shared with the class or a different book) and a pad of Post-its. The groups' task will be to write the text for the book on Post-its, to be stuck on each page. Later the books can be shared with other groups.

It may be helpful to model this activity first with the entire class. Cover up the text in a Big Book with evocative illustrations, then let students make up stories; write them down on large Post-its on each page. Also, since many book covers are beautifully illustrated, they can be used to elicit verbal and written responses in the same manner as a wordless book.

Adaptation
Use this same approach with older students by viewing a soap opera or movie without the sound. Let the students discuss what they think is going on. Then let them dub in the voices or write a short synopsis of the plot.

What to Look for
When discussing the wordless book with children, they should be cognizant of a developing story line.

Puppetry

Instructional Level
Primary – Intermediate (K–6)

Goals
To provide context for English language acquisition; to lower the affective filter by reducing self-consciousness

Explanation
Puppetry can be as simple as using two puppets to converse with each other or as elaborate as performing puppet theater. In one application of this strategy, the teacher talks through a puppet for special purposes or at certain times of day. For example, if the puppet only speaks English, this can cue the children that it's time to switch languages.

Puppetry is an excellent way to make input comprehensible through actions and gestures. Simultaneously, it lowers the affective filter as students' inhibitions melt away. Language learners who are otherwise verbally unexpressive can suddenly become free with words when they hold a puppet. After all, it is the puppet taking all the linguistic risks, not the child!

Examples
Puppets can be made from many simple, everyday materials. Instructions are readily available over the Internet and in books. These are only a few examples of basic puppets that are easily crafted in the classroom or at home: hand puppets, paper-bag puppets, sock puppets, stick puppets, and finger puppets (five per hand).

Materials
- Assorted arts and crafts materials for puppet construction

Guideline
Puppet activities usually occur in two phases: puppet construction, then puppet use.

Extensions
Use puppet construction as an opportunity for an arts and crafts activity that shelters following directions in a second language.

What to Look for
Children should be relaxed and interactive when using puppets to speak in English.

DRAMATIC ARTS 25

Sound Sequence Stories

Response Activity

Instructional Level
Intermediate (4–6)

Goals
To provide context for English language acquisition; to reinforce story structure

Explanation
The teacher describes a short scenario based on daily life, such as getting ready to leave home to participate in a soccer game. In small groups, students create the sequence of sounds from the scenario and record the "track" of their story.

Materials
- Audio recording equipment for each group
- Objects for making sound effects, such as a door closing or an alarm clock; will vary with each group

Guideline
This activity takes place over the course of several days, as students decide which objects they will need to collect in order to complete their recording.

Extensions
Students can write and illustrate the story. The Storytelling with Pantomime strategy on page 22 can then be used as an extension of Sound Sequence Stories.

What to Look for
Although stories will be quite simple, they should still follow a basic story structure that can be understood by the audience.

Folktale Dramatizations

Instructional Level
Intermediate (4–6)

Goals
To provide context for English language acquisition; to reinforce understanding of story structure and narration; to introduce a folktale from another culture

Explanation
A folktale is dramatized through sequential, scaffolded steps. For example:

The entire process begins with the selection of a story appropriate to the interest and linguistic level of the class *(see guidelines on the facing page)*.

The teacher reads the story to students, maximizing the use of dramatic expression, gesture, and illustration to provide comprehensible input. She may ask the students to assist in multiple readings of the story by joining her for repeated refrains and sound effects.

The teacher then leads a discussion about the different scenes in the story. Functioning as the classroom scribe, she writes the scenes in sequential order and displays them prominently in the classroom.

Students volunteer for various roles in the dramatization. Additional roles may be created by using multiple characters (e.g., two cats instead of one) or living scenery (e.g., grass swaying in the wind.) Ideally, a role should be assigned to all students in the classroom to maximize participation, reduce self-consciousness, and lower the affective filter.

The story is enacted one scene at a time, with support from the teacher, who can cue the students when to begin and end each scene or when to chant the story's refrain. (A hand drum is useful as a cueing device.) With each enactment, the dialogue that the students create should become easier.

After the first few enactments, the teacher leads a discussion on how the dramatization might be improved, including what the students liked and what they would propose to change.

Students can be invited to create props, costumes, and scenery to enhance the dramatization, which may be formalized into a theater production with improvised drama. Finally, other classrooms can be invited to view the production.

Materials
- Illustrated folktale
- Props, costumes, scenery (optional)
- Hand drum (optional)

Guidelines

Begin by choosing an appropriate folktale. Some guidelines to consider include:

- Easily discernible story structure
- Simple, repetitive story line
- Spoken refrains that are easily memorized
- Need for animal noises or sound effects
- Appropriate theme
- Opportunities for all students to participate

Shelter language in the storytelling phase and add scaffolding during the dramatization phase.

Keep the emphasis on process even if the activity will culminate in a production. It's better to let students choose the roles they want or for the teacher to make purposeful decisions about roles. Under no circumstances should "auditions" be held, as this will raise the affective filter and put an emphasis on product rather than process. There is also no need to dramatize folktales for performance in front of an audience. Students will find them valuable just for the fun of it.

Extension

Do multiple enactments and allow the students to change roles. This will enable each child to play the role he or she prefers and will maximize language development.

Adaptation

This strategy can be used with "told" stories that are not illustrated in books. In these cases, however, the teacher may want to find illustrations elsewhere to portray concepts or characters, especially when telling the story for the first time.

What to Look for

One advantage of dramatizing folktales through improvisation rather than memorization of a script is the authenticity that results. The final dramatization should have the quality of spontaneous speech. However, there are many things to look for along the way. These include students' participation in the process proportional to their level of English proficiency. Beginning English learners may play parts that require less speech, but they should still be engaged in interpreting their roles. A collaborative spirit is also essential; this activity should be seen as a group effort of the entire class.

Improvisation

Instructional Level
Intermediate – Secondary (4–12)

Goals
To provide context for English language acquisition; to develop empathy and understanding of human behavior; to promote affective change

Explanation
Improvisation (a.k.a. "improv") is the impromptu enactment of scenarios with endings that may or may not be previously determined. When enacted in the classroom, these can be devised either by the teacher or by the students. In second language contexts, however, teachers are best equipped to create the framework for an improvisation. Since students may experience difficulty or embarrassment when speaking impromptu in English, improvisations can be tailored to their linguistic level.

It is essential that students not be asked to participate in an improvisation until they are linguistically ready to do so. Improvisation does not shelter language. Rather, it provides a scaffold that can help move students from sheltered language activities to extemporaneous ones *(see the Preface, pages ix–x, for an example of this type of sequencing).*

Examples
Here are some possible improvisations to try with your students:

Theme: Home
A brother and sister want permission to stay out past the normal curfew to attend a friend's birthday party. They brainstorm about creative arguments to use on their parents.

A brother and sister are at home after school. The brother wants to watch a sports event, and the sister wants to watch a movie that she has been waiting to see for a month. There is only one television in the house.

Theme: School
A student sees his best friend stealing money for the class field trip from the teacher's desk. While speaking with his cousins, he agonizes over how to respond.

A student has just discovered that she is failing a high school class and may not be able to graduate on time. After school she walks to the park and sits down on a bench to think about it. Several of her friends walk by and ask her why she looks so sad.

Theme: Community

A student has a reputation for always arriving late to school. On the weekend of a soccer playoff, the city bus arrives at her stop a full hour late. She misses the most important game of the season and her team loses. On arriving at the game's conclusion, the student tries to explain.

Some high school friends are in a movie theater watching a serious drama. Seated nearby, another group of teenagers is creating a distraction by talking, laughing, and eating popcorn noisily. The two groups interact.

Materials
- Empty space in the classroom
- Movable classroom furniture

Guidelines
Choose situations that are relevant to the lives of your students and fall within the range of their experiences. Avoid situations that could be inherently embarrassing, such as those involving romance, or those that promote superficiality, such as slapstick humor. For improvisation to be authentic, the affective filter must be kept low and the students must believe in what they are doing.

Also remember to keep the scenarios simple because they are in the students' second language.

Extensions
Introduce dilemmas into the improvisation by giving different pieces of information to different characters *(see the example in the Preface, pages ix–x)*.

Have different students try improvising the same scenarios, but with different outcomes. Then discuss the implied options for human behavior.

Have the students write a script *(see page 46)* based on one of their improvisations.

What to Look for
Authenticity is the key. Students should not be "playing at" or stereotyping characters, but should strive for natural, believable reactions to each situation.

Choral Reading

Instructional Level
Intermediate – Secondary (4–12)

Goals
To provide context for English language acquisition; to gain an appreciation of literature

Explanation
Choral reading is a group activity under the direction of a leader (usually the teacher) that is designed to bring literature to life. The selection is read aloud, with a range of choreographed voices. Words can be voiced in unison as an entire group, as a subset of the group, or individually.

Poetry easily lends itself to choral reading, especially when scripted by the teacher to meet the contextual demands of the classroom. Initial discussion of the poem is enhanced by multiple readings for an authentic purpose: the perfection of dramatic impact. Reading simultaneously with others also builds students' fluency and self-confidence. The social nature of choral reading is especially useful in lowering the affective filter for beginning students in a second language.

Example
See the sample script on the facing page.

Materials
- Scripts of a selected poem

Guidelines
A choral reading is usually scripted in voices rather than character names. Assign a number to each student to signify a voice. Use dramatic pauses where appropriate. Multiple readings are helpful not only in achieving dramatic effect, but also in fostering language acquisition.

Extensions
Discuss the meaning and implications of the poem.

Ask students to create their own choral scripts from their favorite poems or from original poems. The teacher or a student can lead the reading.

Have smaller groups of students work on perfecting a choral reading. Then hold an in-class or whole-school performance. Repeat this event for parents on a curriculum night.

What to Look for

The final choral reading, whether recited before an audience or presented only for the participants, should have a dramatic impact, resulting in an enjoyable aesthetic experience.

Excerpt from
"Let America Be America Again"
By Langston Hughes*

1:	The free?
2:	Who said the free? Not me?
3:	Surely not me?
1–3:	The millions on relief today?
1–5:	The millions who have nothing for our pay?
1–7:	For all the dreams we've dreamed
1–9:	And all the songs we've sung
1–11:	And all the hopes we've held
1–13:	And all the flags we've hung,
1–17:	The millions who have nothing for our pay —
1:	Except the dream that's almost dead today.
2:	O, let America be America again —
	The land that never has been yet —
	And yet must be — the land where every man is free.
	The land that's mine — the poor man's, Indian's, Negro's
1–17:	ME —
3:	Who made America,
4:	Whose sweat and blood,
5:	whose faith and pain,
6:	Whose hand at the foundry,
7:	whose plow in the rain,
1–17:	Must bring back our mighty dream again.
1:	O, yes,
	I say it plain,
	America never was America to me,
	And yet I swear this oath —
1–17:	America will be!

*Adapted and arranged for choral reading with 17 voices by Sharon Adelman Reyes

Readers Theater

Instructional Level
Secondary (7–12)

Goals
To provide context for English language acquisition; to gain an appreciation of literature

Explanation
Readers Theater is the oral interpretation of literature adapted for a scripted production. It is minimalist theater that is meant to highlight the original author's voice by keeping the audience focused on the printed word. For this reason scripts are not memorized but read aloud by the performers. Nor is the action staged or choreographed; it is acted out symbolically through gesture and facial expression.

Readers Theater shelters language in multiple ways. Because it emphasizes dialogue, the present tense is used extensively. Dramatic reading allows for the modification of speech through pacing and intonation, as well as gesture and facial expression. Small, symbolic props and costume pieces provide visual and manipulative aids to understanding. As students prepare for performance, they engage in multiple practice sessions. Thus repetition of vocabulary and syntax is authentic rather than contrived, as in grammar exercises.

The hands-on process of creating a Readers Theater production offers multiple opportunities for sheltering English. As always, when using the arts for educational purposes, the emphasis should be on process, not performance. When priority is placed on impressing the audience, superficiality can be the result, with the students "playing at" rather than becoming the characters. Focusing on process, by contrast, fosters a deeper understanding of the characters and the dramatic situations in which they find themselves.

Example
See the sample script from "Rappaccini's Daughter" on pages 34–35; a synopsis of the entire story can be found on pages 119–120.

Materials
- Scripts
- Symbolic props and costumes
- Essential oil spray (optional)
- Musical selection and audio equipment (optional)
- PowerPoint background slides (optional)

Guidelines

Blocking, costumes, and props are minimal. Stage sets, if used at all, are simple and symbolic. Characters are typically seated, usually in a pattern that highlights their relationships to each other. The performance may feature either a single narrator or multiple narrative voices. The script should not be memorized, but kept visible to emphasize the written word. Students should be familiar enough with it to read expressively and occasionally avert their eyes from the page.

Extensions

Turn your classroom into a theater for staging multiple productions. Invite other classrooms to attend, including those with English learners.

Encourage authentic writing in the second language by making a program book for the production. You may want to include historical information about the original story and its author, along with short bios of the performers.

Do informal dramatic improvisations of scenes from the story. This will help your students integrate new vocabulary and syntax into their linguistic repertoire.

When using previously scripted material, read the original story.

When using classic literature, discuss how works such as *Romeo and Juliet* have been updated to become contemporary. Then let the students create a script and a performance transposing a historical story into modern times.

Have students create Readers Theater scripts from additional literary works.

View any existing films of the featured story (many classics have been turned into movies). Contrast the film to the original literature and to the Readers Theater script.

Foster academic language development by discussing issues brought forward by the story. For example, "Rappaccini's Daughter" provokes such questions as: What is ethical in the name of scientific research? and Do ends justify means?

Use technology by creating background slides for various scenes in the production.

Create atmosphere by using aromas *(see page 39)*, dimming the lights, or playing music between scenes.

What to Look for

In the short term, students should understand the Readers Theater story line and connect its theme(s) to their own experiences. The long-term goal of appreciating literature will be more difficult to evaluate. Enjoying the Readers Theater experience, however, will be an important first step.

Excerpt from
"Rappaccini's Daughter"
By Nathaniel Hawthorne*

Giovanni: Dear Beatrice, all is not lost. Look! Here is a medicine a wise doctor gave me. It is made from herbs that are the opposite of your father's poison. Let us drink it together and we will be cured.

Beatrice: Give it to me! I will drink it first. You must wait to see what happens to me before you try it.

Narrator: Beatrice begins to drink from the vial. At the same moment, Rappaccini emerges from house and comes slowly toward the marble fountain. He gazes with a triumphant expression at the young couple, as if he is finally satisfied with his success. When he reaches them he spreads out his hand over them, as if giving a blessing.

Rappaccini: My daughter, you are no longer alone in the world! Pick one of the blooms from your sister shrub, and let your bridegroom wear it on his shirt. It will not harm him now! He now stands apart from ordinary men, as you stand apart from ordinary women. You can now live in this world beloved to one another, and dreadful to all others!

Narrator: Beatrice is becoming weaker and weaker. She speaks with her hand upon her heart.

Beatrice: My father, why did you doom my life to this misery?

Rappaccini: Misery? What do you mean, foolish girl? Do you think you are doomed to have such marvelous gifts, against which no enemy could triumph? Do you think it is misery, to be able to defeat the mightiest person with a single breath? Do you think it is misery to be as terrible as you are beautiful? Would you have preferred to be a weak woman, exposed to all evil in the world and not capable of evil yourself?

Beatrice: I would rather have been loved than feared. But it does not matter now. I am going, father, where the evil you have tried to make part of me will pass away like a dream. The fragrance of these flowers will no longer poison my breath. Farewell, Giovanni! Your words of hatred are as heavy as lead within my heart, but they, too, will pass away. Oh, was there not, from the first, more poison in your nature than in mine?

Narrator: Beatrice sinks to the ground. Her life is poison and the only possible cure is death. And so Beatrice, the poor victim of one man's evil experiment, dies there, at the feet of her father and Giovanni. Just at that moment, Professor Pietro Baglioni looks out of the window. He calls loudly, with horror, to Rappaccini, the man of science.

Baglioni: Rappaccini! Rappaccini! And is this the result of your experiment?

*Adapted for Readers Theater by Sharon Adelman Reyes

Greek Chorus

Instructional Level
Secondary (7–12)

Goals
To provide context for English language acquisition; to gain an appreciation of Greek theater and the role of the Greek chorus in literature

Explanation
The Greek chorus was a homogenous group of performers in the plays of classical Greece. It provided commentary with a single collective voice on the dramatic action occurring before them. Chorus members were similarly costumed and positioned either beneath the stage, at the edge of the stage, or in the orchestra for the duration of the performance.

The chorus was a central feature of Greek drama. Its role was not only to observe and comment but also to add a sense of spectacle, to help the audience follow the performance, to provide time for scene changes, and to give the main actors a break. In ancient Greek theater, the chorus often expressed what the lead actors could not say — their hidden fears, doubts, and secrets. It also provided other characters with insight and moral guidance.

The idea behind this strategy is to adapt the Greek chorus to either a contemporary issue or a literary work with moral and ethical dimensions. Because the lines of the chorus are simple and repetitive, the language is sheltered. Because it is recited as a chorus, the affective filter is lowered, even when the content is sophisticated.

Example
The use of a Greek chorus can be added to a Readers Theater script *(see the facing page)*. But imaginative teachers can add a Greek chorus to many other works, such as an essay or even a newspaper article.

Materials
- Scripts
- Identical robes or fabric coverings for each chorus member (optional)

Guidelines
The script may be developed by the teacher, the students, or all of them collectively. Depending on its complexity, the script may or may not be memorized.

Extension

Develop the work into a performance for another class. Then invite that class to collectively discuss with your own students the moral or ethical issues raised in the performance.

What to Look for

In the short term, your students should show an understanding of the moral significance of the Greek chorus. Of course, it will be more difficult to see evidence of their appreciation of the chorus as a literary device. As in Readers Theater, however, student enjoyment and engagement are first steps toward that long-term goal.

READERS THEATER SCRIPT OF

"RAPPACCINI'S DAUGHTER"

BY NATHANIEL HAWTHORNE

WITH GREEK CHORUS

Giovanni: Dear Beatrice, all is not lost. Look! Here is a medicine a wise doctor gave me. It is made from herbs that are the opposite of your father's poison. Let us drink it together and we will be cured.

Beatrice: Give it to me! I will drink it first. You must wait to see what happens to me before you try it.

Greek Chorus: Don't drink it! Don't drink it! Don't drink it! Don't drink it!

Narrator: Beatrice begins to drink from the vial. At the same moment, Rappaccini emerges from house and comes slowly toward the marble fountain. He gazes with a triumphant expression at the young couple, as if he is finally satisfied with his success. When he reaches them he spreads out his hand over them, as if giving a blessing.

Rappaccini: My daughter, you are no longer alone in the world! Pick one of the blooms from your sister shrub, and let your bridegroom wear it on his shirt. It will not harm him now! He now stands apart from ordinary men, as you stand apart from ordinary women. You can now live in this world beloved to one another, and dreadful to all others!

Greek Chorus: Dreadful, dreadful, dreadful, dreadful!

Narrator: Beatrice is becoming weaker and weaker. She speaks with her hand upon her heart.

Beatrice: My father, why did you doom my life to this misery?

   Greek Chorus: Doom, doom, doom, doom!

Rappaccini: Misery? What do you mean, foolish girl? Do you think you are doomed to have such marvelous gifts, against which no enemy could triumph? Do you think it is misery, to be able to defeat the mightiest person with a single breath? Do you think it is misery to be as terrible as you are beautiful? Would you have preferred to be a weak woman, exposed to all evil in the world and not capable of evil yourself?

   Greek Chorus: Evil, evil, evil, evil!

Beatrice: I would rather have been loved than feared. But it does not matter now. I am going, father, where the evil you have tried to make part of me will pass away like a dream. The fragrance of these flowers will no longer poison my breath. Farewell, Giovanni! Your words of hatred are as heavy as lead within my heart, but they, too, will pass away. Oh, was there not, from the first, more poison in your nature than in mine?

   Greek Chorus: Who really is the poisonous one? Oh yeah! Who really is the poisonous one?

Narrator: Beatrice sinks to the ground. Her life is poison and the only possible cure is death.

   Greek Chorus: Who really is the poisonous one? Oh yeah! Who really is the poisonous one?

And so Beatrice, the poor victim of one man's evil experiment, dies there, at the feet of her father and Giovanni. Just at that moment, Professor Pietro Baglioni looks out of the window. He calls loudly, with horror, to Rappaccini, the man of science.

Baglioni: Rappaccini! Rappaccini! And is this the result of your experiment?

   Greek Chorus: Is this worthy of science? Is this worthy .... worthy .... worthy (fade to silence)

*Adapted by Sharon Adelman Reyes

Aromas to Evoke Mood

Response Activity

Instructional Level
All levels (K–12)

Goal
To enhance context for English language acquisition by creating atmosphere for other activities

Explanation
Aromatherapy involves the use of extracted, highly concentrated oils from plants such as woods, nuts, seeds, resins, herbs, trees, and flowers. The scents of these *essential oils* act upon the limbic system, the structures of our brain that stimulate emotion and long-term memory. The olfactory effects can be intense, impacting mood by creating and renewing feelings associated with particular scents.

Thus aroma can be especially evocative in providing context for dramatic arts strategies, such as Folktale Dramatizations *(pages 26–27)* and Readers Theater *(pages 32–35)*.

Examples
See pages 114 and 122 for aromatherapy recipes that can be used for evocative purposes in the dramatic arts.

Materials
- Essential oils
- Water
- Spray bottle

Guidelines
Essential oils should be mixed and used only by the teacher. For maximum effect, she should spray the scents into the air when the students are not in the room or when the lights are dimmed.

Be alert to the potential hazards of using certain essential oils, including allergic reactions, as summarized on page 40.

What to Look for
Students should remark on a different scent in the air, although they may not know specifically what it is. The teacher can pick up on student commentary by saying things like, "Hmmmmm, it smells like grassland in Africa," or "It reminds me or a garden of pungent, exotic flowers."

ENGAGE

Warning

Essential oils are highly concentrated, so it is best to use a carrier such as water for spray. Sprays have a lesser impact than applications, but in higher concentrations they can cause irritation. Never substitute synthetics, because they can be toxic.

Be careful to avoid the essential oils listed below, which can cause allergic reactions for some people. *Always be vigilant for any special health concerns of individual students.*

**ESSENTIAL OILS
WITH A PROVEN OR SUSPECTED HISTORY OF
CAUSING SENSITIZATION**

- Aniseed
- Bay
- Benzoin
- Balsam of Peru
- Calamus
- Cardamom
- Cassia (use at low concentrations)
- Cinnamon Bark & Leaf (use at low concentrations)
- Citronella
- Fennel
- Fig Leaf Absolute
- Galbanum Resin (when used with Peru Balsam)
- Hyacinth Absolute
- Jasmine Absolute
- Junipers
- Laurel (bay laurel)
- Lemon (suspect)
- Litsea Cubeba (suspect)
- Lovage (suspect)
- Mimosa Absolute
- Oakmoss Concrete (suspect)
- Orange (suspect)
- Pines (suspect)
- Rose Absolute (if used in high concentrations)
- Spearmint
- Tolu
- Tagetes
- Balsam
- Lemon Verbena
- Ylangylang (if used in very high concentrations)

Creative Writing

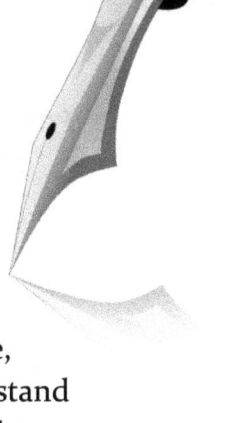

A word after a word after a word is power.
　　　　　　　　　　　　　Margaret Atwood

CREATIVE WRITING PUTS US IN TOUCH with mystery, suspense, intrigue, adventure, and discovery. Once your students understand the power of mind and pen, they can go virtually anywhere. The creative writing strategies included in this section feature stories, scripts, and poetry.

Across time and cultures, *storytelling* has become a universal human activity. In fact, we seem to be "wired" for creating and listening to stories. They entertain us, of course. But more importantly, stories offer ways to share knowledge and preserve cultural values. They can also make us more empathetic and understanding of the lives of others. Stories come in all varieties, from myths and legends to fables, trickster tales, ghost stories, and epic adventures. Because of their universality and motivational ability, stories are a natural choice for creative writing with English learners.

Scripts are another appropriate form because they help to shelter language by reducing linguistic complexity. Besides using the present tense for the most part, they are meant to be enacted or read dramatically (aided by symbolic props, if possible). And their inherently social nature maximizes peer support when read aloud.

Structured poetry works especially well with second language learners. It serves to shelter and scaffold both written and spoken language by providing templates in which students can feel safe expressing themselves. Beginning to create and enjoy their own poems prepares English learners to write less structured poetic forms. Related strategies include Rap and Jazz Chants *(see pages 47–51 and 66–67).*

CREATIVE WRITING STRATEGIES*

Primary (K–3)
- Sentence Stems 43

Primary – Intermediate (K–6)
- Wordless Books 23
- Acrostic Poems 44

Intermediate (4–6)
- Musical Interpretation 61

Intermediate – Secondary (4–12)
- Improvisation 28
- Choral Reading 30
- Process Writing of Stories 45
- Script Writing 46
- Collage 87
- Digital Photo Essay 88
- Mind Maps 90
- Calligraphy 92

Secondary (7–12)
- Readers Theater 32
- Greek Chorus 36
- Rap 47
- Self-Portraits 93
- Multimedia Essay 96

All levels (K–12)
- Structured Poetry 52
- Jazz Chants 66
- Book Arts 99
- Books, Books, Books! 102

*Including cross-listings from Dramatic Arts, Music and Rhythm, Visual Arts, and Free Reading.

Sentence Stems

Instructional Level
Primary (K–3)

Goals
To provide context for beginning English language acquisition; to introduce the writing of poems and stories

Explanation
A sentence stem is a partially complete statement. It typically features a subject and a predicate, followed by a blank for students to fill in. A series of sentence stems, begun by the teacher and completed by a student, can create a beginning-level poem or story.

Example
Students can create a poem About Me by using these sentence stems.

I am _____.	I am José.
I can _____.	I can play.
I can _____.	I can share.
I can _____.	I can listen.
I am _____.	I am your friend.

Materials
- Paper and pencil or pen
- Sentence strips (optional)

Guideline
Sentence stems should be completed in a tense that the learner is comfortable using.

Extension
Illustrate the poem or story with a drawing or a collage.

Adaptation
More complex sentence stems are useful with older students and can be used as a warm-up to the Self-Portraits strategy on page 93.

What to Look for
The finished poem or story makes sense as a coherent whole (unlike a collection of unrelated sentences) and has meaning to the child.

Acrostic Poems

Instructional Level
Primary – Intermediate (K–6)

Goals
To provide context for English language acquisition; to introduce descriptive writing

Explanation
An acrostic poem uses the first letter of each line to spell out a word or phrase in a vertical format. A common way to begin is to highlight a student's first name. Because acrostic poems can be short and do not need to rhyme, they are easy for English learners to write.

Example
*J*umping
*O*kay
*E*nergy

Materials
- Paper and pen or pencil

Guideline
The teacher should specify whether the poem will use only specific parts of speech, such as adjectives and adverbs, or whether all that matters is the theme.

Extension
If students are ready, the acrostic poem can be expanded to use phrases rather than single words, for example:

*J*umping high
*O*kay to fly
*E*nergy to go

Adaptation
Have students compose acrostic poems about themselves, which can be used as warm-ups to the Self-Portraits strategy on page 93.

What to Look for
The finished poem or story makes sense as a coherent whole (unlike a collection of unrelated sentences) and has meaning to the child.

Process Writing of Stories

Instructional Level
Intermediate – Secondary (4–12)

Goals
To provide context for English language acquisition; to experience success in writing

Explanation
Process writing is a series of scaffolds, each leading seamlessly from one phase of composition to the next, with plenty of support from peers. The sequential stages usually consist of prewriting (such as brainstorming), drafting, revising, editing, and publishing. Process writing encourages students to draw on their own experience, thus validating prior knowledge. Cooperative assistance is provided by peers (usually in small groups) in the form of ideas, suggestions, critiques, and feedback during each phase of the process. Editing is attempted only when revisions are complete, so that students can focus on creativity and meaning. Then comes publishing. While mainstream students do not need sheltering, they can benefit as much as English learners from the scaffolding that process writing provides.

As language "output," writing does not cause language acquisition; only comprehensible input does that. But, as Krashen points out, "it helps solve problems and makes us smarter."

Materials
- Paper and pen or pencil

Guideline
Due to its social nature, process writing requires all group members to observe some protocols. These can be developed by the full class. They should stress constructive criticism and suggestions that promote the writer's self-confidence and enjoyment of writing.

Extensions
Students can illustrate their own stories or the stories of others. Working in teams as authors, illustrators, and graphic designers helps them understand the collaborative nature of book production.

Stories can be published through Book Arts techniques *(see page 99)*, either individually or in classroom anthologies.

What to Look for
Writing group members should be respectful of each others' work and take it seriously. Final stories should be interesting and exhibit an appropriate level of technical competence.

Script Writing

Instructional Level
Intermediate – Secondary (4–12)

Goals
To provide context for writing in English; to develop empathy

Explanation
Script writing shelters English by using everyday language and staying mostly in the present tense. When done in small groups, it provides peer support both for generating ideas and for composing the script.

This strategy encourages students to explore real-life interpersonal dilemmas, either inside or outside of school, as the basis for writing a script. In the beginning, this can take the form of one-act scripts. After students become adept at the activity, it can extend into longer scripts with more intricate problems and solutions.

Materials
- Paper and pen or pencil

Guideline
This is meant to be a stand-alone activity in creative writing. Students may choose to turn it into a drama performed by themselves or others, but that is optional.

Extensions
To jump-start students' thinking, show a soap opera without the sound track and discuss what they think is going on in the episode. Then write a script to go along with the action *(see adaptation on page 23)*.

Use this activity as a way to test solutions for real problems. If the solutions seem to have potential, try them outside of school. Then come back and discuss the results.

Publish the scripts in a classroom anthology.

What to Look for
Students should improve their writing skills while becoming more introspective and empathetic in dealing with interpersonal dilemmas.

Rap

Instructional Level
Secondary (7–12)

Goals
To provide context for English language acquisition; to appreciate and create poetry; to understand poetry as a contemporary and relevant art form

Explanation
Rap is poetry set to a musical beat. Grounded in popular culture, it often has immediate appeal for adolescents. Rhyming lyrics are chanted to musical accompaniment and performed in time to an insistent, recurring rhythm. Rap is heavily dependent on lyrics and has a strong background in improvisational poetry. Topics can include human relationships, community happenings, current events, and literature *(see example on pages 125–126)*.

Contrary to popular belief, rap is also a highly structured musical form. Its reliance on patterned lyrics makes it a form of structured poetry as well. Due to the complexity of that structure, however, it is most appropriate for use with secondary students. Because of its strong dependence on lyrics, rap can be intellectually challenging and cognitively stimulating.

At first glance, these rhyme forms may seem too sophisticated for many English learners. Yet, when students are highly motivated, they often surprise us with what they can do. In this sense, rap provides an introduction to a wide variety of poetic forms and styles.

The appropriate use of rap as a classroom genre illustrates for students how language can be both relevant and playful and that word play is enjoyable. And remember — it's all about the lyrics.

Materials
- Handouts on rhyme, metaphor, and structure of a rap *(see pages 48–51)*
- Sample audio recordings with written transcript of lyrics
- Metronome (to help students maintain the beat)
- Electronic keyboard or other musical equipment for base beat

Guidelines
Appearances can be deceiving; rap is a complex genre. You should not attempt to incorporate rap into your classroom without some technical grounding in this contemporary art form. A brief introduction follows.

Parts of a Rap

- *Intro:* The section that opens the rap and establishes its rhythm.

- *Verses:* The main parts of the rap, which correspond to poetic stanzas.

- *Hook:* The part of the rap that contains its themes and makes it memorable. The hook corresponds with a musical chorus and is often greater in musical and emotional intensity than the verses.

- *Breakdown:* A section in which the rap is deliberately reduced to minimal elements, usually the percussion or rhythm.

- *Outro:* The ending, or passage that brings the rap to an end, which corresponds with a musical coda.

- *Bridge:* An optional transition near the end of the rap, usually occurring only once, that is musically and lyrically different from the rest of the rap. For example, C in ABABCAB.

Structure of a Rap

The typical length of a rap verse is 16 bars, with each bar corresponding to one sentence. Thus a 16-bar rap verse should have 16 sentences. The duration of a rap is typically about four minutes and contains two or three verses. Here are some examples of rap structure:

Three-Verse Rap Song

Intro — 8 bars

Verse 1 — 16 bars

Hook — 8 bars

Verse 2 — 16 bars

Hook — 8 bars

Verse 3 — 16 bars

Hook — 8 bars

Outro — 16 bars, but can be 32 bars or longer, depending on whether the rapper has something he or she would like to say over the outro.

Three-Verse Rap Song with Breakdown

Intro — 8 bars

Verse 1 — 16 bars

Hook — 8 bars

Verse 2 — 16 bars

Hook — 8 bars

Verse 3 — 16 bars

Breakdown

Hook — 8 bars

Outro — 16 bars, but can be 32 bars or longer, as needed

Two-Verse Rap Song

Intro — 8 bars

Verse 1 — 24 bars

Hook — 8 bars

Verse 2 — 24 bars

Hook — 8 bars

Outro — 16 bars, but can be 32 bars or longer, as needed

Simplified Rap Structure for Beginning Classroom Use

Hook — 8 bars, or 4 bars repeated *(see example on pages 125–126)*

Verse 1 — 16 bars

Hook — 8 bars, or 4 bars repeated

Verse 2 — 16 bars

Hook — 8 bars, or 4 bars repeated

OPTIONAL RHYMING FEATURES

Metaphor and rhyme are central features of rap lyrics. Most teachers are familiar with metaphor and perfect rhyme *(true/blue, mountain/fountain)* but there are many other rhyming forms to use with students, as described below.

Multisyllabic rhymes ("multies") are phrases in which more than one syllable rhymes. The following examples, as well as ideas for teaching multisyllabic rhymes, can be found at chasemarch.blogspot.com/2011/02/teaching-tip-multi-syllable-rhymes.html.

Multisyllabic rhymes for a cold winter day:

- Old spinsters pray
- Gold winners play
- The old sinister man from the bay
- Fold printer paper this way
- Polled the Prime Minister today
- Bold tornado lays destruction

Multisyllabic rhymes contrasted to a normal rhyme:

- Normal rhyme — *cat / hat*
- Multi rhyme — *my cat / hi-hat*
- Longer multi rhyme — *bit my cat / hit the hi-hat*

Internal rhyme occurs within a line or a passage, either at random or in a pattern, for example, as in Edgar Allan Poe's poem "The Raven":

> *Once upon a midnight dreary, while I pondered, weak and weary,*
> *Over many a quaint and curious volume of forgotten lore —*
> *While I nodded, nearly napping, suddenly there came a tapping,*
> *As of someone gently rapping, rapping at my chamber door.*
> *"'Tis some visiter," I muttered, "tapping at my chamber door" —*
> *Only this and nothing more.*

Slant rhyme (a.k.a. imperfect rhyme, half rhyme, approximate rhyme, near rhyme, off rhyme, or oblique rhyme) is close but not exact, such as *dark/heart*. Here is a slant rhyme used in a poem by Emily Dickinson:

> *Hope is the thing with feathers*
> *That perches in the soul,*
> *And sings the tune without the words,*
> *And never stops at all.*

Identical rhyme is created by repeating a word, for example: *stone/stone*.

Rich rhymes are homonyms that rhyme with each other: *blue/blew, guessed/guest*.

Assonant rhyme has similar vowels and different consonants: *dip/limp, man/prank*.

Consonant rhyme has similar consonants and different vowels: *limp/lump, bit/bet*.

Macaronic rhyme uses more than one language and offers an excellent opportunity to explore bilingual poetry. Students soon discover they can create more rhymes when they have a larger supply of rhyming words to choose from. For example, *con* (English) and *pan* (Spanish).

Suggested Process for Creating a Rap

- Select a topic and a beat.
- Select a structure *(see the options on pages 48–49, among others)*.
- Write the hook, or chorus, containing the theme of the rap.
- Write the verses; each verse should be 16 bars.
- Use metaphors, an effective way to convey complex concepts succinctly.
- Rap and refine. Practice rapping in the chosen beat (a metronome may be helpful). Refine the written verses. If desired, add a pause or two to emphasize an important point in the rap.
- Memorize the rap.
- Produce (record) or perform the rap.

Extensions

Have students create raps on topics of relevance, along with musical accompaniment and movement if possible.

Enable them to create their own music video, then share it with the class.

Hold an evening Rap Fest (similar to a Poetry Slam) and invite the school community.

What to Look for

The finished rap should adhere to structural guidelines and have some musicality. The artistry of the rap will be evident in the quality of the lyrics such as rhyme scheme and use of metaphor.

Structured Poetry

Instructional Level
All (K–12)

Goals
To provide context for writing in English; to build appreciation of poetry

Explanation
Structured poetic forms can be successful with English learners because they function as literary scaffolds. Rhyming verse may present a particular challenge for students with limited English vocabulary, and free verse may prove too intimidating. Structured poetry, on the other hand, offers opportunities for creative success while helping students acquire English.

Although we usually think of structured poems as appropriate for use with younger children, in reality they can be effective at many grade levels. That's because, while the structure remains unchanged, the content is dependent on context. Simple poetic forms can express complex ideas, scaffolding both cognitive and linguistic development. *(To explore how structured poetry can be adapted to content, see page 123.)*

There is a multitude of structured poetic forms, easily obtainable in print or over the Internet. Teachers can engage students in the poetic form best suited to their English proficiency level, or they can offer a choice of forms. Publishing student work in a poetry anthology creates further incentives for writing, as do illustration and choral reading.

Materials
- Paper and pen or pencil

Guidelines and Examples
See the facing page.

Extension
Have students write and publish their own poems and poetry anthologies, incorporating artwork and using book-making techniques.

What to Look for
Poems should follow the correct structure and express a coherent idea.

Haiku

The *haiku* is based on a syllabic pattern expressed in three lines that convey a single idea. The first line contains five syllables, the second contains seven syllables, and the third contains five syllables.

Flowers are blooming
Yellow, red, orange, purple
The earth comes to life

Haikon

The *haikon* is a pictorial representation of the haiku. For example, the poem above could be converted into a haikon by drawing the outline of a flower and writing the words around its shape.

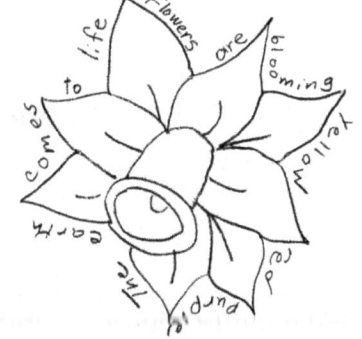

Tanka

The *tanka* adds two more lines to the haiku, each containing seven syllables.

Flowers are blooming
Yellow, red, orange, purple
The earth comes to life
In colors that invite me
To go into the garden

Terquain

The *terquain* uses structure — three lines on a single subject — without a rigid syllabic formula. So it offers even a primary-level English learner the chance to be a successful poet. The first line consists of a one-word noun. The second line describes the noun in two or three words, and the third line is either a synonym for the noun or describes a feeling about it.

Soccer
Kicking, running, punting
Happiness

Cinquain

The *cinquain* also uses structure without a rigid syllabic formula, but it's a bit more sophisticated. The first line is a noun. The second line uses two words to describe the noun. The third line contains three action verbs that describe the noun, while the fourth line contains four words that describe feelings about the noun. The fifth and final line consists of one word that is synonymous with the noun used in the first line.

Dog
Warm, furry
Bark, jump, run
Care, share, sad, happy
Friend

Diamante

The *diamante* combines grammatical structure with pictorial form in seven lines. It splits thematically in the fourth line, so that the first half of the poem is conceptually the opposite of the second half of the poem. It is graphically represented in a diamond shape.

Day
warm, light
run, jump, play
school, park, sofa, bed
sleep, snore, dream
cool, dark
night

As illustrated above, the first line consists of one word, a noun, and the last line is its opposite. The second and sixth lines contain two adjectives that describe the respective nouns. The third and fifth lines contain three action verbs each, and the fourth (middle) line is split, with two nouns referring to each opposing concept.

Music and
Rhythm

If I were not a physicist, I would probably be a musician. I often think in music. I live my daydreams in music. I see my life in terms of music. I get most of my joy in life out of music.

Albert Einstein

MUSIC BRINGS MELODY AND RHYTHM TO THE CLASSROOM. It creates mood, inspires movement, and promotes careful listening. In addition, its potent link to memory makes music an ideal medium for oral language development. Songs stay in our minds long after we stop singing them. So they can help us acquire vocabulary, syntax, and the rhythm of language simply by engaging in an activity we enjoy.

But that's not all. Music affects our energy level, our feelings, and our frame of mind. It can evoke powerful memories, help us to focus, or sooth us into relaxation. Music can play both practical and symbolic roles, from signaling transitions between classroom activities to strengthening the bonds between students and teacher. By enriching everyday life, it sets the scene for important experiences and contributes to making school a place we want to be.

The strategies in this section include rhythmic games, chants, songs, and musical response activities. *Rhythmic games* and *chants* lower the affective filter when students begin using their second language. *Songs* often incorporate gesture and movement, sheltering and providing a natural scaffold for language acquisition.

Because music is such a potent emotional trigger, it is ideal for use as a *response activity.* In addition, exposing students to various musical genres enhances their appreciation of possibilities for artistic expression.

Music and Rhythm Strategies*

Primary (K–3)
- Play Party Songs 57
- Infinite-Loop Motif Chants 58
- Drumbeat Statues 71
- Choreographed Dance Songs 73
- Songs with Pantomime 74

Primary – Intermediate (K–6)
- Teacher-Adapted Songs 60
- Visual Journey 82
- Classroom Transformation 85

Intermediate (4–6)
- Musical Interpretation 61

Intermediate – Secondary (4–12)
- World Music Journey 63

Secondary (7–12)
- Rap 47
- Student-Adapted Songs 64
- Dance Interpretation 77
- Self-Portraits 93
- Multimedia Essay 96

All levels (K–12)
- Jazz Chants 66
- Books, Books, Books! 102

*Including cross-listings from Dramatic Arts, Creative Writing, Dance and Movement, Visual Arts, and Free Reading.

Play Party Songs

Instructional Level
Primary (K–3)

Goals
To provide context for English language acquisition; to promote multicultural appreciation

Explanation
Play party songs are part of the African-American musical tradition, used to accompany children's games. The repetition, rhythm, and movement shelter language, while the rules of the games provide a linguistic scaffold. There are three basic types of play party songs:

- *Ring games.* These are played in a circle formation. Sometimes a child with a special role may be stationed in the center. Examples: Little Sally Walker; Miss Lucy; Loop De Loo; Bluebird, Bluebird; and Go In and Out the Window.

- *Line games.* These are played in two lines. Sometimes children pair up to dance or to complete other motions. Examples: Here Comes Sally and Climb the Mountains.

- *Clapping rhymes.* These are usually played in pairs, with the children facing each other. Rhythmic patterns are performed using various clapping techniques (hand to hand, hand to thigh, two hands, one hand, diagonally, straight across, etc.) to accompany the words. The clapping patterns can be changed by the players and are often quite elaborate. Examples: Mary Mack; Hambone; and Down, Down, Baby.

Guideline
Each song accompanies a game with specific rules.

Extensions
Discuss the African-American origins of play party songs with your students.

Turn play party songs into a classroom tradition. Perform the class favorites at birthday parties or during other special classroom events.

What to Look for
Students maintain the beat, perform the required motions, and sing the song with ease.

Resource
Shake It to the One That You Love the Best: Play Songs and Lullabies from Black Musical Traditions, collected and adapted by Cheryl Warren Mattox (JTG of Nashville, 1990).

Infinite-Loop Motif Chants

Instructional Level
Primary (K–3)

Goal
To provide context for English language acquisition through chanting

Explanation
In an infinite-loop motif chant, each verse feeds directly into the next. The chant is usually performed in a circle and often includes clapping or finger-snapping. It features call-and-response, a musical genre with roots in West Africa and the Deep South. A variation, the infinite-loop motif game, includes the same verse structure but without singing, chanting, or clapping. It does, however, emphasize repetition reinforced by rhythm, which serves to shelter the second language.

Guidelines
These chants and games are typically performed with the children seated in a circle on the floor. They can also be done in a circle of chairs. The teacher will need to create a predetermined signal to end the activity or it could go on indefinitely.

Examples
"Who Stole the Cookies" is an infinite-loop motif chant with clapping:

> All of the children sit in a circle and clap in rhythm to the chant. The clapping sequence can be simple or elaborate. A suggested starting point is to clap both hands together, then against both thighs. The teacher should make sure that all children get a chance to do solo parts.
>
> *Entire Group: Who stole the cookie from the cookie jar?*
>
> *Accuser: (name of the accused child) stole the cookie from the cookie jar.*
>
> *Accused: Who, me?*
>
> *Accuser: Yes, you!*
>
> *Accused: Couldn't be!*
>
> *Accuser: Then who?*
>
> The game then repeats, with the accused taking on the lines of the accuser and naming another child.

"I Give You" is an infinite-loop motif game without clapping:

> The teacher sits with the children in a circle. She holds an object in her hand. In the example below, a glove is used.
>
> *The teacher turns to the person seated to her right (Child A) and says: I give you a glove.*
>
> *Child A looks at the teacher and asks: A what?*
>
> *The teacher replies: A glove.*
>
> *Child A takes the glove from the teacher, saying: A glove.*
>
> *Child A then turns to the next child seated to the right (Child B) and says: I give you a glove.*
>
> *Child B looks at Child A and asks: A what?*
>
> *Child A turns and looks at the teacher, who started it all, and says: A what?*
>
> *The teacher replies: A glove.*
>
> *Child A turns to child B and says: A glove.*
>
> *Child B says: A glove.*
>
> *Child B then turns to the next child seated to the right (Child C) and says: I give you a glove.*
>
> The pattern continues until it involves each child in succession, returning to the beginning of the circle.

Extension
Change the words as desired. For example, the word *stole* could be changed to *took*, forming the question *Who took the cookies from the cookie jar?* Or change *Couldn't be!* to *Not me!*

What to Look for
After an initial learning curve, there should be no breaks in the rhythm of the chant or game.

Teacher-Adapted Songs

Instructional Level
Primary – Intermediate (K–6)

Goal
To provide context for English language acquisition through adapted song lyrics

Explanation
By adapting the lyrics, teachers can create songs to fit their classroom context, as well to shelter language so that the songs are more comprehensible to the students.

Example
See the Primary Unit on page 109.

Materials
- Audio equipment and CD or DVD (optional)
- Piano, guitar, autoharp, or other musical accompaniment (optional)

Guidelines
Keep the song's original rhythm and melody.

Change the syntax and vocabulary to make it comprehensible to the students.

Change the words to fit the context of the learning activity.

Extension
Add hand and arm motions to fit the lyrics of the song.

What to Look for
Children should be able to pick up the lyrics quickly if the song has been adapted for their level of language proficiency.

Musical Interpretation

Response Activity

Instructional Level
Intermediate (4–6)

Goals
To provide context for English language acquisition; to promote appreciation of instrumental music

Explanation
First, students listen to an evocative symphony or overture. Then the teacher presents the actual narrative that goes with the musical work while it plays in the background.

Examples
The symphony *Peter and the Wolf* was composed by Sergei Prokofiev in 1936, a classic illustration of storytelling for children through music. All of the characters have a musical theme, which makes it especially easy to understand the story. Recordings of *Peter and the Wolf*, with narration included, are widely available. The story follows.

> One day Peter goes out into the clearing, forgetting to shut the garden gate. This allows a duck to leave the yard and go swimming in a nearby pond. The duck argues with a little bird: "What kind of bird are you if you can't swim?" The little bird responds, "What kind of bird are you if you can't fly?" Meanwhile, Peter's pet cat silently stalks both the duck and the bird. Peter sees this and warns both fowls just in time for them to escape.
>
> Peter's grandfather scolds him for leaving the yard: "Suppose a wolf came out of the forest?" But Peter declares, "Boys like me are not afraid of wolves." So his grandfather takes him back inside the house and locks the gate.
>
> A wolf soon comes out of the forest. All of the animals escape except the duck, who is swallowed by the wolf. After witnessing this, Peter climbs over the garden wall into a tree and ultimately catches the wolf. Hunters who have been tracking the wolf arrive. Peter convinces them not to shoot the wolf, but instead to take it to the zoo. All the characters then leave in a victory parade to the zoo, with the grandfather grumbling, "What if Peter hadn't caught the wolf? What then?"

62 ENGAGE

The *Sorcerer's Apprentice* is a symphony by Paul Dukas, composed in 1896–97 and based on a poem (a ballad in 14 stanzas) of the same name, written in 1797 by Johann Wolfgang von Goethe. Recordings of *The Sorcerer's Apprentice* are also readily available. The story follows:

> An old sorcerer goes out, leaving his apprentice in charge of his workshop. The apprentice grows tired of doing his menial chores and decides to use magic to accomplish them. He enchants a broom to do his work — fetching water with a pail — by using magic in which he is not fully trained. The broom quickly finishes its task, but the apprentice does not know how to stop the broom from fetching water. In frustration, he splits the broom in two with an axe, but then each of the pieces becomes a new broom. Both brooms take a pail and continue fetching water, which now accumulates at twice the speed as before. The apprentice becomes frantic. But just when all seems lost, the old sorcerer returns and breaks the spell, declaring that powerful spirits should only be called by the master himself.

Materials
- Audio equipment and CD or DVD

Guideline
The emphasis should be on visualizing the story told by the symphonic music, not on creating original stories to accompany it.

Extensions
Create a wordless book of the story.

Write a structured poem about a character or event in the story.

Create a dance or movement sequence to go along with the music.

Dramatize the story through pantomime.

What to Look for
Student engagement should be evident through students' focused listening; it can also be seen through one of the responses suggested in the Extensions above.

World Music Journey

Response Activity

Instructional Level
Intermediate – Secondary (4–12)

Goals
To provide context for English language acquisition; to see past stereotypes about human diversity and recognize the connections between peoples

Explanation
The teacher takes students on an imaginary journey to different regions and countries through music she has previously recorded or collected. When the selections are complete, the teacher asks the students to guess their places of origin.

Examples
The idea is to expand students' knowledge about and appreciation of diversity, so intriguing selections are important. Sephardic songs in the Ladino language or Afro-Peruvian rhythms are good examples. Regions of the United States can be represented with music such as Zydeco, Tejano, or Hawaiian.

Materials
- Audio equipment and CD or DVD

Guidelines
Ground rules need to be established in advance concerning how and what kinds of answers may be offered. One option is to have students write down their guesses on paper, rather than calling them out. The teacher can tally the responses on the board to look for patterns in response, then ask the students what criteria they used to make their choices.

Extensions
This strategy can be used as a motivational device when beginning the study of another country or culture.

The teacher can ask students to list the countries whose music they would like to study.

What to Look for
Students should exhibit curiosity about different musical forms and the cultures from which they come.

Student-Adapted Songs

Instructional Level
Secondary (7–12)

Goal
To provide context for English language acquisition through rewriting song lyrics

Explanation
Students change the lyrics of a popular song to fit a topic they are studying in class or one that interests them. Note that the adaptation is done by students, not by the teacher. This is different from the strategy *(see page 60)* in which the teacher does the adapting to fit the instructional context she has planned.

Example
See the facing page.

Materials
- Paper and pen or pencil
- Percussive instruments (optional)

Guideline
This activity is most successful when based on student choice, and popular songs provide strong incentives to create inventive adaptions.

Extensions
Add percussive instruments as back-up rhythm for the song.

Adaptations
Use this strategy in an interdisciplinary way. Create theme songs for characters in a book, or about historical events.

What to Look for
The lyrics should make sense and fit the rhythmic structure of the original song.

MUSIC & RHYTHM 65

Excerpt From
"I Just Wanna Fly"
By Sugar Ray

All around the world statues crumble for me
Who knows how long I've loved you
Everywhere I go people stop and they see
Twenty five years old
My mother, God bless her soul

Adaptation
"I Just Wanna Grow"
By an 8th Grade Bilingual Student

All around the world people look down on me
Who knows how long I've suffered
Everywhere I go they are taller than me
Milk will make me grow
My mother, she told me so

Jazz Chants

Instructional Level
All (K–12)

Goals
To provide context for English language acquisition; to use simple language that is relevant and appropriate for the learner, while internalizing the sound system of a language

Explanation
Carolyn Graham, the creator of jazz chants for use in teaching English, defines them as "poems with repeated beats" that use language that is real, useful, and appropriate for the learner. They are the "rhythmic expression of spoken American English [that can be used as] a way of learning to speak and understand with special attention to the sound system of a language."

As their name suggests, jazz chants originated with the musical genre of jazz, which in turn can be traced back to the West African musical style that incorporates polyrhythms (the simultaneous combination of contrasting rhythms), syncopation, improvisation, and call-and-response. Jazz chants are frequently used in English learner classrooms because they use the motivational elements of movement and rhythm to scaffold the syllable stress and intonation of conversational American English.

Graham became interested in jazz chants when she realized that "the sound of spoken language reflects exactly the rhythm of traditional American jazz." It made sense to her to use jazz chants to teach English, because doing so "brought rhythm into the classroom, and the brain loves rhythm." She points out that rhythm and memory are closely linked, noting that "a student can easily memorize any material if you present it with rhythm."

Today jazz chant competitions are held throughout the world. Many of these teacher- and student-created routines are easily accessible on YouTube. As can be seen by the diverse ages of the competitors, jazz chants are enjoyable to students from primary through secondary school.

Materials
- None required; costumes and props optional

Guidelines
Jazz chants frequently incorporate hand-clapping, foot-stamping, and simple body movements; so they involve kinesthetic as well as musical memory. They use elements of

both music and movement to make language learning fun, while encouraging the internalization of language.

One caution, however: Be careful not to let this activity turn into the kind of repetitive grammar drills used in the "audio-lingual method" of language teaching.

Among the many teacher resources that Graham has published, here is one of her ideas for creating jazz chants:

- Begin with a topic and a four-beat rhythm.

- Select three words on that topic. The first word should have two sounds, the second word should have three sounds, and the third word should have one sound. (Graham calls this the magic formula of 2-3-1.)

- Add pronouns, plus a verb.

- Add a yes-or-no question and a short response.

Example
Does she paint pictures?
Yes, she does.
Does he write poetry?
Yes, he does.
Do they dance?
Yes, they do.

Extensions
Add musical accompaniment and movement.

Add costumes, props, and scenery.

Let students create their own jazz chants on relevant topics.

Stage a jazz chant festival in your classroom or at your school.

What to Look for
In addition to maintaining a jazz beat, the students should be using language that is real, useful, and appropriate for everyday purposes.

Resource
Carolyn Graham's website: jazzchants.net/who-is-carolyn-graham/.

Dance and Movement

Dancing is the loftiest, the most moving, and the most beautiful of the arts. For it is no mere translation or abstraction of life. It is life itself.
  Havelock Ellis

MOVEMENT CREATES A FORM OF RESPONSE AND RELEASE without having to make a sound. Kinesthetic awareness engages our bodies as well as our minds in the learning process. And appreciation of the many forms of dance gives us a deeper understanding of nuance, culture, and the possibilities for self-expression.

This section includes activities in creative movement and dance appreciation. *Creative movement* can be especially useful as a response activity with students in the early stages of second language learning. For that reason, it is extensively used in the Total Physical Response model of ESL. An additional advantage is its potential to reinforce students' listening skills. Comprehensible input can be maximized when stories and songs are interpreted through movement and dance. Involving students in the *interpretation of formal dance compositions* also provides opportunities for engaging them in discussion.

Cross-listed strategies in other creative arts add extensions to this section. Movement and dance are fundamental components of activities such as jazz chants and rap, heightening their motivational qualities. And pantomime brings the dramatic arts into the realm of creative movement. Although dance may sometimes be difficult to incorporate into intermediate and secondary classrooms, its links to so many other art forms create opportunities to tap the kinesthetic possibilities of learning.

Dance and Movement Strategies*

Primary (K–3)
- Storytelling with Pantomime 22
- Play Party Songs 57
- Drumbeat Statues 71
- Choreographed Dance Songs 73
- Songs with Pantomime 74

Primary – Intermediate (K–6)
- Teacher-Adapted Songs 60

Intermediate (4–6)
- Storytelling through Movement 76

Secondary (7–12)
- Rap 47
- Dance Interpretation 77

All levels (K–12)
- Jazz Chants 66
- Books, Books, Books! 102

*Including cross-listings from Dramatic Arts, Creative Writing, Music and Rhythm, and Free Reading.

Drumbeat Statues

Response Activity

Instructional Level
Primary (K–3)

Goals
To provide context for English language acquisition through movement; to promote careful listening; to work on gross motor skills

Explanation
The teacher beats a rhythm on a hand drum and the children move to the beat. Whenever she stops beating, they must freeze in position — like statues.

After students have mastered this activity, the teacher can add movement instructions, for example, skipping, leaping, running in place, falling down, hopping on two feet, or hopping on one foot. The teacher beats the appropriate rhythm on the drum. As before, at the moment the drum stops beating, the children must freeze in position.

Next the teacher can ask them to move like certain animals and insects, again making the appropriate rhythmic accompaniment on the drum. The classroom is transformed into a menagerie of animals such as snakes, lions, birds, and butterflies.

Descriptors may be added for each of the animals called out. For example, the lions can stalk and the butterflies can flutter.

Materials
- A hand drum and drumstick *(for an illustration, see page 26)*

Guidelines
All of the children participate at the same time. The teacher can add rules as needed, such as no physical contact between individuals.

Extensions
Half of the group moves to the drumbeat, with children deciding which animal each would like to be. When the drum stops beating, they freeze into poses representing their respective animals. Meanwhile, the other half of the class moves from one "animal statue" to the other, trying to guess what it is. When they guess correctly, the statue can unfreeze. If the class cannot guess, eventually the teacher can unfreeze the statue with a tap of the drum stick, and let the animal reveal its identity. The groups then switch roles, so that all students get a chance to become an animal statue.

72 ENGAGE

Extensions (cont'd.)

Each child has a partner. One becomes a lump of clay while the other must shape the "clay" into an animal statue. When the statue gallery is complete, all of the sculptors convene with the teacher. Moving from statue to statue, they attempt to guess what animal has been crafted. As before, the teacher holds the power to bring the statue to life with a touch of the drum stick. Ask the children to switch roles so that all have a chance to be both sculptor and clay.

What to Look for

It is essential that the children stop moving immediately when the drum beat stops, and that they adhere to any classroom rules for the game. This is a matter of simple safety. A benefit of this game is that, once mastered, the hand drum can be used to restore calm and quiet in many different classroom situations.

The students should not all select the same few animals. If that occurs, the class should step back from the activity and review the different options that are available.

Choreographed Dance Songs

Response Activity

Instructional Level
Primary (K–3)

Goals
To provide context for beginning English language acquisition through movement

Explanation
Singing songs accompanied by hand movements is a common practice in early childhood education. A classic example is the traditional nursery song "The Incy Wincy Spider." So is a predefined choreography of song and dance, such as the "Hokey Pokey." Choreographed movement is an excellent way to shelter language, and there are many possibilities for teachers to create their own dance songs. Children struggling to find their own words in a second language also appreciate the structure afforded by the chorus.

Example
"Let's Make Some Noise," as sung by Raffi, lends itself easily to this activity. The upbeat Caribbean rhythm and contagious melody frame lyrics that invite children to move. The song can be performed in a circle, like a folkdance, with students holding hands and moving to the right or left. The teacher can choreograph sound and motion to correlate with the lyrics of the song.

This is a good way to start the day in a primary classroom. Energy is expended but controlled. When the dancing is finished, students can usually settle down for more sedentary activities.

Materials
- Audio equipment and CD or DVD

Guideline
In advance of the activity, the teacher invents choreography for the dance, using the lyrics to structure the movement.

What to Look for
The children should perform the dance in the choreographed pattern. Singing along is desirable but not required.

Excerpt from "Let's Make Some Noise"

Sing something high
sing something low
sing something joyful
sing it round and round

Clap something once
clap something twice
clap something happy
clap it right out loud

Shake something left
shake something right
shaking and dancing
move it round and round

Songs with Pantomime

Response Activity

Instructional Level
Primary (K–3)

Goal
To provide context for beginning English language acquisition through movement and music

Explanation
While listening to an audio recording of a song, children pantomime its action. The purpose of the activity is not singing, but listening and responding to the lyrics. If singing happens naturally, however, it should not be discouraged.

Example
Many children's recording artists have produced songs with potential for this activity. Raffi's songs are especially evocative in this regard, as illustrated by the opening verse of "In My Garden":

> *Digging, digging*
> *This is how we dig the ground*
> *In our garden, in our garden*
> *Digging, digging*
> *This is how we dig the ground*
> *Early in the morning*

Each subsequent verse continues the action: *This is how we hoe the weeds, This is how we plant the seeds, This is how the peas will grow, This is how we'll pick the peas,* and finally ending with *This is how we'll eat those peas.*

Materials
- Audio equipment and CD or DVD

Guidelines
Let the children listen to the song while seated the first time it is played, encouraging them to sway with the music. Then join them in pantomiming the song's actions and movements. Choose songs without multiple roles so that all students can pantomime in unison.

DANCE & MOVEMENT 75

Extension

Find children's poems on the same topic as the song. Have students pantomime the poem without background music. In effect, this removes one of the scaffolds (music) and encourages the appreciation of poetry.

An example of a poem that would combine nicely with "In My Garden" is *Wild Wild Sunflower Child Anna*. Because this poem takes the form of a picture book, the language is sheltered visually. Listening to it read aloud while viewing the illustrations will prepare students to do the pantomime. Here is an excerpt:

> *Digging in the garden*
> *kneeling on her knees,*
> *leaning on her elbows*
> *whispering to the seeds.*
> *Anna sifts the soil*
> *lightly through her fingers.*
> *Anna talking, Anna walking*
> *sunshine.*
> *Grow, grow*
> *grow in the garden Anna*

What to Look for
The students' movements should follow the story line.

Resources
For information on songs and poems to use with this activity, see page 131.

Storytelling through Movement

Response Activity

Instructional Level
Intermediate (4–6)

Goals
To provide context for beginning English language acquisition through movement; to reinforce story structure

Explanation
Working in small groups, students create a simple story based on a movement sequence. After each group performs its sequence for the rest of the class, the other students discuss what they think the short story was about.

Materials
- Props (optional)

Guideline
Neither musical accompaniment nor words are allowed unless they are being used as an extension of the original activity.

Extensions
Students write and illustrate the story that they created through movement.

Students add a soundtrack to the story they created, thus creating a dance composed out of the abstraction of everyday movement.

The Sound Sequence Stories strategy *(see page 25)* can be used as an extension of Storytelling through Movement.

What to Look for
There should be a logical sequence of movement.

Dance Interpretation

Response Activity

Instructional Level
Secondary (7–12)

Goals
To provide context for English language acquisition; to gain appreciation of dance genres

Explanation
The class watches a video that tells a story or portrays a theme through a particular dance genre, such as modern dance or jazz dance. After breaking into small groups to discuss their interpretations, students share their thoughts with the larger group. The goal is not to guess the "correct" interpretation of the dance, but to imagine and to share. In the final phase, if there was a predetermined story line, the teacher shares it with the class.

Examples
Appalachian Spring, a well-known composition by Aaron Copland, premiered in 1944 and shortly thereafter was choreographed by the modern dancer Martha Graham. Clips of her work, based on the lives of American pioneers of the 19th century, are readily available on the Internet. The story features the spring festivities that celebrate the completion of a Pennsylvania farmhouse. The central characters include a newlywed couple and a revivalist preacher and his followers

The Alvin Ailey Dance Theater features a more contemporary dance style. Clips from *Revelations* are readily available online. This acclaimed production uses African-American spirituals, song-sermons, gospel songs, and blues to explore "the places of deepest grief and holiest joy in the soul."

Pilobolus is a modern dance company that explores many ways of using the human body as a medium of expression. Such choreography often centers on theme and imagery rather than story, and can be a potent trigger for student imagination. Clips of Pilobolus dance compositions are also widely available.

Materials
- Dance video and video equipment

Guideline
It is best to use instrumental music only. If there are lyrics, as in *Revelations,* keep the focus on interpretation of movement. This should not be difficult, as movement tends to be more immediately comprehensible; it also creates a scaffold for student discussion.

Extensions

Storytelling through Movement *(see page 76)* can be used as a warm-up activity for this strategy.

Like *Appalachian String* and *Revelations,* many professionally choreographed dance compositions make excellent connections to social studies, much like a historical novel. Use them to create interdisciplinary units.

Compare a short dance to a poem. Write a structured poem about the dance composition that the class has viewed.

Take students on a field trip to see a professional dance concert. Afterwards, discuss the performance. Focus on questions such as: Was there a story line or was the dance thematic? What were the connections to culture? To history? To contemporary life?

What to Look for

The interpretations shared by the students should be plausible and not stated merely for laughs.

Resources

See page 131 for dance websites.

Visual Arts

I found I could say things with color and shapes that I couldn't say in any other way — things I had no words for.
                                        Georgia O'Keeffe

LEARNING BECOMES TACTILE as we use our hands to fashion artifacts. It becomes visual as we experiment with color and form. And it becomes richer as we gain an aesthetic appreciation of what others have created and what we can create on our own.

The strategies in this section incorporate arts and crafts, visual response, book arts, and activities that enhance our experience of other creative arts. For students in the beginning stages of second language acquisition, many of the visual arts can function as Total Physical Response activities by providing rich context for the teacher's directions and comments.

Arts and crafts projects are especially useful in this regard because they provide lots of comprehensible input and require little or no output whatsoever. They also allow students to walk away with a lovely artifact, thus enhancing motivation for the project.

Visual response activities work in a similar manner. Mind maps, collages, drawings, and murals give students an alternative to verbalizing their thoughts. Conversely, for more advanced English learners, such activities can trigger a multiplicity of verbal responses.

The visual arts can be used as activities that enrich other creative arts forms. The *book arts* — leading to the production of an actual physical book, including calligraphy and illustrations — can extend and maximize strategies in drama and creative writing. And the creation of props, costumes, scenery, and puppets are natural compliments to music, dance, and the dramatic arts.

VISUAL ARTS STRATEGIES*

Primary (K–3)
- Wordless Books 23
- Sentence Stems 43
- Simple Arts and Crafts 81

Primary – Intermediate (K–6)
- Puppetry 24
- Acrostic Poems 44
- Visual Journey 82
- Illustration 84
- Classroom Transformation 85

Intermediate (4–6)
- Folktale Dramatizations 26
- Musical Interpretation 61
- Origami 86

Intermediate – Secondary (4–12)
- Process Writing of Stories 45
- Collage 87
- Digital Photo Essay 88
- Mind Maps 90
- Calligraphy 92

Secondary (7–12)
- Self-Portraits 93
- Tape Resist Art 94
- Multimedia Essay 96

All levels (K–12)
- Structured Poetry 52
- Murals 98
- Book Arts 99
- Books, Books, Books! 102

*Including cross-listings from Dramatic Arts, Creative Writing, Music and Rhythm, Dance and Movement, and Free Reading.

Simple Arts and Crafts

Instructional Level
Primary (K–3)

Goals
To provide context for beginning English language acquisition; to learn to follow directions

Explanation
Many simple arts and crafts activities, by asking students to follow directions in the second language, provide excellent sources of comprehensible input. Teachers can demonstrate how to create the particular craft, while giving verbal instructions one step at a time.

Examples
Countless arts and crafts activities are suitable for children at this level and are readily available over the Internet or in craft books. Some examples include:

- Paper-weaving
- Tissue paper flowers
- Egg carton caterpillars
- Basic origami
- Simple dream catchers

Materials
- As needed for specific projects

Guidelines
Choose activities that require step-by-step instructions, but still allow for some individual choice. In paper-weaving, for example, the children may choose their own colors, the size of the paper strips, and so on. When working with origami *(see page 86)*, choice can be offered in color and size of paper. While more free-flowing projects, such as clay sculpture, are worthwhile, they provide fewer opportunities for students to listen carefully in their second language and demonstrate their understanding by following directions.

Extensions
Decorate the classroom with student-made arts and crafts or use them in the classroom.

For children at the intermediate level, more advanced crafts can be created and simple instructions can be written instead of demonstrated.

What to Look for
The finished crafts should demonstrate an ability to follow directions.

Visual Journey

Response Activity

Instructional Level
Primary – Intermediate (K–6)

Goals
To provide context for English language acquisition; to focus attention on the settings of stories, novels, or historical places and events

Explanation
The teacher takes his students on an imaginary journey to a different time or place. As a first step, he may ask them to close their eyes while he plays evocative music or sound effects. Afterwards, he asks the children what images were evoked by the music.

The children close their eyes again, but this time the teacher uses the recording as a background track as he describes in vivid terms the place to which they are "traveling." Then the recording is replayed while they draw what they have imagined.

Finally, the teacher may compare student drawings to professional renditions or photographs of the place they have visited in their imaginations.

Materials
- Audio equipment and CD or DVD
- Paper and drawing supplies (pencils, charcoal, crayons, etc.)
- Narrative script for the teacher (optional)

Guidelines
Rather than telling students what to draw, the teacher should use music and dramatic descriptions to evoke a mood to inspire their imaginations. The children's drawings are not expected to replicate the teacher's pictures and photographs, but some elements should be similar. If they are not, the class can discuss why, contrasting the two sets of images. Either way, a sense of wonder can be created around a different time or place that can be used to encourage further investigation or to stimulate interest in an upcoming lesson or unit.

Extensions
Try adding aroma to the mix. If students journey to a lavender field in the French countryside, the teacher can spray the scent of lavender into the air. Mixes of essential oils with water can produce a multitude of scents such as fir trees or citrus fruits *(see pages 39–40)*.

Experiment with light and darkness to produce the appropriate mood for an imaginary journey. Not only the classroom lights, but window blinds and flashlights can produce desired effects.

Adaptation

With older students, the techniques of producing a distinctive mood with sound, light, and scent can be used effectively in Readers Theater productions and in improvisations.

What to Look for

This activity is designed to stimulate students' curiosity about other times and places, which should be reflected in their enthusiasm for an upcoming unit or additional research projects.

Illustration

Response Activity

Instructional Level
Primary – Intermediate (K–6)

Goals
To provide context for English language acquisition; to assess students' level of comprehension; to enhance children's graphic abilities

Explanation
Encouraging students to draw pictures is such a simple activity that it's often considered trivial. But it can be important when working with second language learners. When children draw what they hear, see, experience, think, and feel, they can let the teacher into their world without being forced to provide linguistic output.

Examples
As a response activity, students at a beginning level of English proficiency can illustrate a story told by the teacher.

Students can also use illustration to:

- Express aspects of their family life
- Give input on how to deal with classroom situations
- Reveal an understanding of the curriculum
- Respond to local, national, or world events

Materials
- Paper
- Illustration tools (pencils, pastels, charcoal, watercolor paints, crayons, etc.)

What to Look for
When children illustrate a story told by the teacher, elements of their drawings will reveal their levels of comprehension. That information will assist the teacher in adjusting his level of English input. Illustrations can also supply valuable knowledge about how the students live and what they know, thus guiding other instructional decisions.

Classroom Transformation

Instructional Level
Primary – Intermediate (K–6)

Goals
To provide context for English language acquisition; to virtually transport the students to another time and place

Explanation
The classroom space is redesigned to make it visually suggestive of the subject matter being studied. This can involve putting scenic backdrops on the walls, rearranging the furniture, hanging objects from the ceiling, making huts or small boats from rolls of heavyweight paper, using fabric to create streams, and so on.

This strategy can be used to enhance literature, science, and social studies units.

Materials
- Art and other supplies as needed

Guideline
Students should work in cooperative groups to complete various tasks related to the classroom transformation.

Extensions
Visit a museum of natural history that has exhibits replicating other environments, regions, or historical eras. Use this as a way to generate ideas for transforming your classroom.

Experiment with the following elements to create a stronger transformational effect:

- Aromas *(see pages 39–40)*
- Sound effects such as those recorded from nature
- Instrumental music
- Light and darkness (e.g., using flashlights, lamps, curtains, and window shades)

What to Look for
The transformed classroom should evoke the mood of the time and place being studied.

Origami

Instructional Level
Intermediate (4–6)

Goals
To provide context for English language acquisition; to learn to follow directions

Explanation
Origami is the ancient Japanese art of paper-folding. It was popularized outside of Japan in the mid-1900s and has subsequently evolved into a modern art form. In origami, a flat sheet of paper is transformed into a finished sculpture through folding and sculpting techniques. Cutting and gluing are not permitted, making origami easy to use in the classroom.

Paper used for origami comes in various sizes and is square in shape. Often it features a solid color or multicolored design on one side and white on the other. While many types of origami paper are available for purchase, all that is really needed is a square sheet. Better yet, a white sheet and a colored (or multicolored) sheet can be glued back-to-back. It is a good idea, however, to purchase a book on origami with helpful directions.

Examples
Origami creations can take many forms. Here are a few to start with: hat, cup, Valentine, furniture (bed, chair, or table), bird (crane or pigeon), and animal finger puppet (cat, dog, fish, alligator, snail, rabbit, or frog).

Materials
- Origami paper, either store-bought or adapted

Guideline
The teacher gives verbal instructions while demonstrating each paper fold.

Extensions
Make an origami mobile or hanging ornament. Because it is lightweight, it moves easily and without a strong support, so it can be hung almost anywhere in the classroom.

Origami creations can be used with other classroom activities, such as a life-size hat to accompany a Japanese folktale. Or hats could be used to celebrate birthdays or other events.

What to Look for
The finished product should look like the teacher's creation, given some leeway to account for students' dexterity.

Collage

Response Activity

Instructional Level
Intermediate – Secondary (4–12)

Goal
To provide context for English language acquisition through visual expression

Explanation
A collage is a form of abstract art in which pictorial and textual representations of recognizable objects (such as photographs, pieces of paper, newspaper cuttings, and pictures cut from magazines), are placed in juxtaposition and glued to a surface, often a piece of paper. When arranged artistically in this fashion, a unique work of art with a new meaning is created by the collective use of other materials.

Students who are not able to participate fully in verbal discussion of a given topic can express what they have understood through the creation of a collage.

Examples
Create a collage on a topic such as family, future professional interest, nature, or friends, or on a concept such as fairness, beauty, justice, or war.

Materials
- Paper and glue
- Pictorial and textual representations of objects

Guideline
Once the appropriate materials have been gathered, students should be allowed sufficient time to complete this activity independently.

Extensions
Students can create an oral or written artist's statement to explain their collage.

Collages about self can be combined with the following strategies: Sentence Stems *(page 43)*, Acrostic Poems *(page 44)*, Mind Maps *(page 90)*, and Self-Portraits *(page 93)*.

What to Look for
The student should use the collage form effectively to communicate a theme.

Digital Photo Essay

Response Activity

Instructional Level
Intermediate – Secondary (4–12)

Goals
To provide context for English language acquisition; to interpret the natural or social environment through photography

Explanation
As part of a science or social studies unit, students take and artistically arrange a series of digital photographs. Such projects enable students to demonstrate both the factual knowledge they have acquired and a deeper understanding of the topic.

Photos can depict subject matter wherever appropriate — in the classroom, school, home, or community.

The photographic display may be presented in various ways, such as an album, book, collage, poster, website, PowerPoint presentation, or exhibit.

Examples
Possible topics may include:

- The plant world, such as woodlands, crops, and gardens
- The animal world, such as insects, pets, farm animals, and wild animals
- Earth science, such as bodies of water, grasslands, and mountains
- Social phenomena, such as immigration and the lives of immigrants
- Aspects of culture, such as family life, celebrations (Cinco de Mayo, El Día de los Tres Reyes Magos, Chinese New Year, etc.)

Materials

- Digital or cell phone cameras, batteries, and charger
- Color printer and inkjet cartridges
- Photo editing software
- PowerPoint or other presentation software
- Book- and album-making materials and equipment (optional)
- Picasa free software for posting, editing, and sharing photographs on Google's Picasaweb site (optional)

Guidelines

Allow students enough time to practice and gain skill in digital photography before attempting any projects. Discuss the difference between taking random photos and using photography to express ideas and concepts.

It may be necessary to provide a system for students to check out digital cameras to use outside of class. However, cell phones can also be used, minimizing the need for the school to purchase special equipment.

Extensions

Photo essays can focus on a wide variety of additional topics, such as explorations of self and family, documentation of field trips or class activities such as experiments and dramatizations, and stories by the students or others.

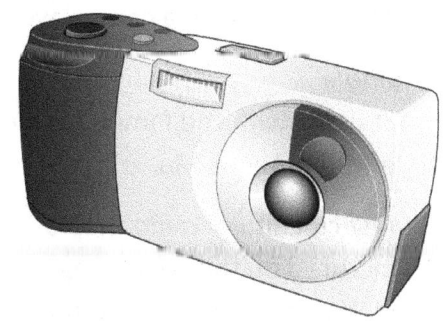

Explanatory text may be added, as appropriate. For example, a collage might only require a title, but an exhibit would need a series of labels for each photograph or group of photographs. A photo album could benefit from lots of text. Or it could be a largely wordless book, depending on students' writing proficiency and ability to convey meaning through visual images.

Student work could be shared with the school and the community. For example, photo albums and books might be displayed in the school library. Or a photography exhibit could be located in the main hallway at times when the school is hosting an event that is open to outsiders.

Adaptation

Explore the same concepts through video clips.

What to Look for

Students should demonstrate knowledge and understanding of the topic being studied, as well as an ability to experiment with artistic elements such as darkness and light, composition, and form.

Resource

Two ESL teachers in Fairfax County, VA, Michelle Campiglia and Sharon Alayne Widmayer, provide useful advice for using digital photography in the classroom at: www.soundsofenglish.org/Presentations/SnapshotsfromLifehandout.pdf.

Mind Maps

Response Activity

Instructional Level
Intermediate – Secondary (4–12)

Goals
To provide context for English language acquisition; to give visual display to a cognitive process

Explanation
A mind map is a visual display of information. Associated words, ideas, and concepts radiate out from a central word, idea, or concept.

Example
Starting with the familiar is a good way to begin, so have your students create a mind map entitled About Me.

A sociocultural mind map by an 11th grade student, a recent immigrant from Mexico, is pictured on the facing page. At the top is a basic, wordless mind map; at the bottom is an elaborated version with text.

Materials
- Paper and drawing supplies

Guidelines
A mind map should expand as it is being created. Brainstorming should happen not just beforehand but throughout the process. Students at low levels of English proficiency do not need to supply text.

Extensions
Sentence Stems and Acrostic Poems *(see pages 43 and 44)* can be used as warm-up activities for About Me, and Self-Portraits *(see page 93)* can be used as a follow-up activity.

Mind maps can also be used effectively in other disciplines, such as science and social studies.

What to Look for
It is the thought behind the drawing, not the graphic sophistication, that matters most.

Mind Map

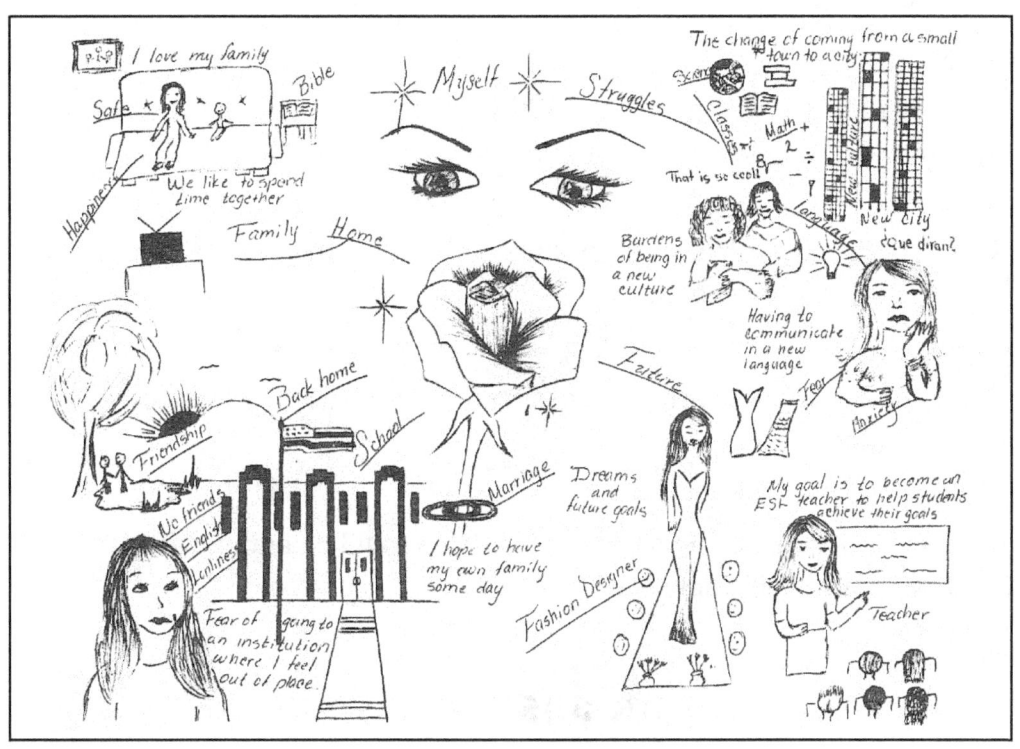

Calligraphy

Instructional Levels
  Intermediate – Secondary (4–12)

Goal
  To provide context and motivation for writing in English

Explanation
  Calligraphy, derived from the Greek word for "beautiful writing," is visual art produced in simple strokes by a broad-tipped instrument or brush. It is usually cursive, though sometimes angular. At first glance, producing calligraphic writing may seem intimidating. But it is actually easy to get started. Calligraphic magic markers in various colors are readily available. So are books offering instruction in calligraphy, as well as guides for beginners on the Internet.

  Calligraphy is one of the book arts, and it can be successfully integrated into book-making projects *(see page 99)*. But it can be used in many other ways, such as producing invitations to classroom events or writing short poems. When completing such projects, special paper can add additional aesthetic dimensions.

Materials
- Paper (varying in weight, color, and texture)
- Calligraphy tools (markers or pens and ink)

Guideline
  Allow students enough time to practice and gain skill in the art of calligraphy before attempting any writing projects.

Extension
  Use calligraphic fonts for artistic purposes *(see example below)* when creating word-processed documents.

What to Look for
  Students' motivation to complete class projects should be enhanced as they seek an outlet for their new calligraphic skills.

Calligraphy means 'beautiful writing'

Self-Portraits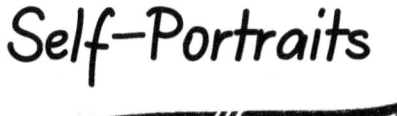

Response Activity

Instructional Level
Secondary (7–12)

Goals
To provide context for English language acquisition; to experience self-discovery through art

Explanation
A self-portrait is traditionally a representation of the artist that is drawn, painted, photographed, or sculpted. In this strategy, a self-portrait is used to show how students' experiences and feelings may be reflected in their art work.

Materials
- Writing and art supplies as needed

Guidelines
Pick the warm-up activities that seem most appropriate for your students, for example:

- Guide them in discussing topics such as what they enjoy doing, whether they prefer to do these things alone or with friends, and what makes them happy or sad.
- Write a poem with the sentence stem "I am … " *(see adaptation on page 43)*.
- Discuss images that students would choose to express their personalities.
- Research examples of self-expressive art, such as self-portraits of Vincent Van Gogh, photography by Ansel Adams, protests songs of the 1960s, or Woody Allen movies.

Use a form of graphic art to create a self-portrait. Since some students lack confidence in their drawing ability, suggest other options such as photography, collage, clay sculpture, and mobiles. Or experiment with another creative arts medium, for example, structured poetry or an arrangement composed of excerpts from several pieces of music.

Extension
Create a self-portrait from the perspective of another person, such as a character in a work of literature, or an important historical figure.

Make an interdisciplinary connection by exploring the life and times of Frida Kahlo, an artist best known for her self-portraits.

What to Look for
The process of self-exploration is more important than the finished product, but students should put serious effort into creating a work that they feel proud of.

Tape Resist Art

Response Activity

Instructional Level
Secondary (7–12)

Goals
To provide context for English language acquisition; to explore and portray the natural world

Explanation
Resist techniques in art create layered effects with color and texture by using two incompatible media. For example, when watercolor paints are brushed over wax crayons, the wax repels the paint, creating interesting colors and textures on the paper.

Tape resist art is based on this same principle. Strips of masking tape are placed on a paper in a geometric pattern. The spaces between the strips are filled in with colors, designs, or other visuals. When the tape is removed, the blank spaces can be filled with another color.

In this variation, the empty spaces are filled with representations of a specific natural environment, such as the Amazon Rain Forest or the Grand Canyon. The example on the facing page (and excerpted on the cover of this book) portrays the Columbia River Gorge.

Materials
- Paper
- Masking tape (or another easily removable tape)
- Media for adding color (crayons, paints, pastels, inks, colored pencils, markers, etc.)

Guidelines
This activity works well with life science or geography units. English learners who lack the confidence to write about what they have learned can communicate their impressions visually while simultaneously creating a work of art.

Extension
Use pieces of photographs, magazine pictures, greeting cards, or other premade visual representations, cut to the correct size, to fill in the spaces between the masking tape.

What to Look for
Students should be attentive to the details of a natural environment, especially in terms of color and texture. This should be reflected in the final piece of art, while at the same time creating an object that can be appreciated aesthetically.

VISUAL ARTS 95

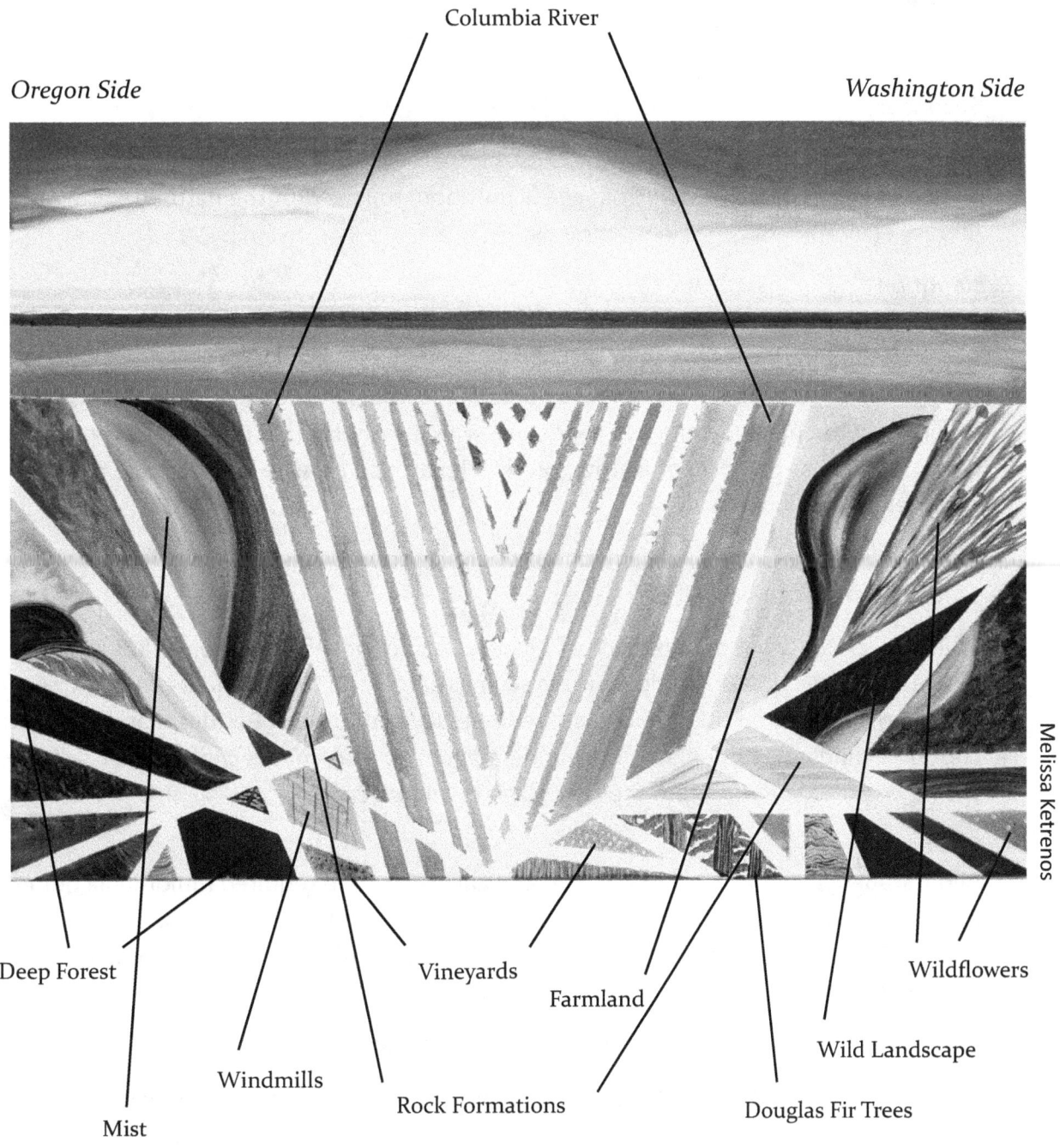

Multimedia Essay

Instructional Level
Secondary (7–12)

Goals
To provide context for English language acquisition; to interpret the natural, social, or literary environment through multimedia

Explanation
As part of a science or social studies unit or the study of a literary work, students create an essay via multimedia (such as photos, video, sound, and text). These technologies enable second language learners either to demonstrate factual knowledge they have acquired or to interpret the meaning of a poem or story, with minimal verbal or written output. When this activity takes the form of a group project, it can also provide a rich source of comprehensible input.

Multimedia essays depict subject matter wherever appropriate — in the classroom, school, home, or community.

Students use software or apps such as I-Movie (Apple) or Movie Maker (Windows) to edit movies and slide shows; to add features such as animation, visual effects, music, oral narration, and written titles; and to share the essay with others. Besides mastering their chosen technology, students need to understand how their media choices are combined with the text to communicate their message to an audience.

Guidelines
Allow students enough time to practice and gain skill in the required multimedia before attempting any projects. Teach students how to use I-Movie or Movie Maker, depending on which program your district has available. Both of these programs enable the user to sequence pictures, superimpose text, add oral narration of text, and include music.

Compare and contrast digital writing with nondigital writing.

Show students an example of a multimedia essay. Ask them to analyze how it is shaped by the media choices of the writer. For some compelling examples, visit the Center for Digital Storytelling: www.youtube.com/user/CenterOfTheStory/videos?flow=grid&view=1.

Have students share their essays with classmates and other audiences, for example, by posting on YouTube or on a class website.

Examples
- Explanations of scientific observations or experiments
- Portrayals of historical or current events
- Biographies of important historical or literary figures
- Mini-documentaries
- Interpretations of literary works

Materials
- Computers or tablets
- Software as noted above
- Digital photos and pictures
- Microphones and headphones

Extension
Once students become proficient in I-Movie or Movie Maker, they may make films on topics such as: My Autobiography, A Day in the Life of… , or A Life-Changing Moment.

What to Look for
Students should use the chosen media, first, to demonstrate knowledge and understanding of the content being studied, and second, to communicate their message and evoke responses from an audience.

Technology Tips

- Ask the technologist in your school to make sure the required software you need is installed and checked for any "barracudas" (tools to block certain websites).
- Make sure that any videos, pictures, and graphics reproduced by students are in the public domain or used with permission of the copyright holder. Ask the technologist to guide you to sites fitting your district's criteria.
- Students may also use photos from their cell phones or prints that can be scanned. Consider taking photos throughout the year and making them available to the students for their projects.
- Adding oral narration will require audio recording and editing tools, which are available free for both Apple (www.apple.com/education/podcasting) and Windows (audacity.sourceforge.net).
- Test all technology before students are scheduled to visit the computer lab, and try to anticipate any glitches students may have with hardware or software.
- *Most importantly, remember that, just as pen and paper are tools for communicating, so is technology. The teacher's role is to help students integrate these tools so that creation of the message can take center stage.*

98 ENGAGE VISUAL ARTS 98

Murals

Response Activity

Instructional Level
All (K–12)

Goal
To provide context for English language acquisition through cooperation in visual arts

Explanation
A mural is any piece of artwork that is painted on or applied directly to a large permanent surface, such as a wall or ceiling. Wall murals may be either inside or outside of a building. Ideally, there should be visual and architectural harmony between the mural and the surface on which it is painted or applied.

Creating a mural can be a visual response to a classroom topic, incorporating different pictures that are thematically related. From planning to execution, it provides opportunities for student participation and for integrating academic content from other disciplines.

Materials
- Drawing, painting, and coloring supplies as needed

Guidelines
Before beginning this project, explore the work of muralists throughout history, from Diego Rivera to your own neighborhood artists. If possible, take a walking tour of a community or visit a museum to see actual murals. At minimum, bring in art books to exhibit murals in your classroom.

What to Look for
Students should have communicated a theme through visual representation. They should be more alert to murals in their own cities or neighborhoods.

"Let Peace Blossom," Konawaena High School, Kealakekua, HI (2009)

Book Arts

Instructional Level
All (K–12)

Goals
To provide context for English language acquisition; to motivate students to create books and appreciate them as art objects

Explanation
Book-making is an art form in its own right. Artists have been active in printing and book production for centuries, but *artist's books* are a late 20th-century form. Often published in small editions, these are sometimes produced as one-of-a-kind objects known as "uniques."

The book arts combine a wide range of formats and crafts. Students of all ages can be involved in book-making, since formats can be as simple as a scroll or accordion book made from a single sheet of paper or as complex as a hand-bound volume with embossed pages. Book crafts related to production — paper-making, graphic design, typography, calligraphy, book-binding, and printing — can also be adapted to varying skill levels.

Book-making can be incorporated into many arts-based activities relevant to second language learners. Students can choose from several options, including wordless books, anthologies, and single volumes. The books they create may be kept in a classroom or school library or displayed for the school community at special events.

Materials
- See Resources for book-making, page 132

Guidelines
It is helpful to provide physical examples of hand-crafted books for students to read and handle before they begin. Adequate time needs to be allotted for crafting the physical book itself, not just for creating the work (both visual and literary) that it will feature.

Extensions
Take students on field trips to institutions that have displays on the traditional arts of printing and typography; examine book-making across cultures and across time.

What to Look for
Although book-making results in a physical product, when applied in the classroom the emphasis should be on the learning process. Thus an appreciation of books and a motivation to create them are the most important outcomes of this activity.

Free Reading

*The man who does not read books has no advantage
over the man who can't read them!*

Mark Twain

DONALYN MILLER, A 6TH GRADE TEACHER, was initially disappointed when she encouraged her students to read independently. Their response was less than enthusiastic. Still, she refused to give up. Consulting with other educators and seeking out professional books, Miller was determined to discover how to pass on her own reading addiction to her students. Ultimately, these efforts paid off. In *The Book Whisperer*, she describes a host of creative strategies that she developed along the way.

Miller was strongly influenced by the ideas of Stephen Krashen, an advocate of free reading as a way to acquire academic language. In *Free Voluntary Reading*, he cites studies that "provide overwhelming evidence that reading for pleasure — that is, self-selected recreational reading — is the major source of our ability to read, to write with an acceptable writing style, to develop vocabulary and spelling abilities, and to handle complex grammatical constructions." What's more, Krashen says, "the evidence holds *both* for English as a first language and for English as a second and foreign language."

In her quest to lead students "toward their autonomy as literate people," Miller discovered that reading "is both a cognitive and an emotional journey." And she realized that, when students have control over what they choose to read, their journey becomes even more successful.

With these principles in mind, I offer suggestions in this section on how to integrate the cognitive experience of reading with the emotional experience of the arts. The books should be chosen by the students, either individually, in partners, or in small groups. Rather than elaborate strategies, these are simple response activities, encouraging students to describe their immersion in a satisfying book.

Books, Books, Books!

Response Activity

Instructional Level
All levels (K–12)

Goals
To develop academic language in English; to create independent, lifelong readers

Explanation
Assign your students to select books and read them individually, with partners, or in small groups. Ask them to respond to the aesthetic experience of reading through one or more of the response activities listed below. Or use the suggestions on page 105 to create your own.

Dramatic Arts
- Dramatize, through improvisation *(page 28)*, a part of the book that is meaningful to you.
- Create a movie trailer of the book.
- Do a Readers Theater performance of the book or a portion of it *(page 32)*; as an option, supplement it with a Greek chorus *(page 36)*. Combine these with the scriptwriting activity below.

Creative Writing
- Write a Readers Theater script of the book or part of the book; as an option, adapt it with a Greek chorus script.
- Capture the theme of the book, the essence of an important character, or the viewpoint of such characters in a poetic form *(pages 47 and 52)*.

Music and Rhythm
- Select an instrumental music sound track for the book (perhaps in combination with a movie trailer).

Dance and Movement
- In subgroups, create a dance or movement sequence expressing the theme of the book.

Visual Arts
- Illustrate the book *(page 84)*.
- Create a mural or collage based on the book *(pages 87 and 98)*.
- Create a mind map for an important character in the book *(page 90)*.
- Create a self-portrait that could have been done by an important character in the book *(page 93)*.

Guidelines

All readers should be excited about the book they have chosen. If any of the students or groups feel they have made a poor selection, they should be allowed to put it aside and choose another book. This might involve a reconfiguration of independent reading groups within the class; that's perfectly acceptable. It is also appropriate for students to read books on their own. Not all of the response activities need to be completed by a group; many are easily adapted for individual use.

What to Look for

Enjoyment and appreciation of literature.

Part III
Sample Units

As a second language teacher, you have many options. After all, language is everywhere, and that means sheltering and scaffolding can be applied in just about any subject area. So why not begin by tapping into your own creative resources? If your passion is music, find a way to integrate music with teaching English. If it's visual art or drama or dance, do the same. Your students will find your enthusiasm contagious. Then expand outward into new fields.

By all means, don't limit yourself to the strategies in this book. Create your own! Here are some guidelines for doing so. First, remember to stress process over performance. Second, choose activities:

- that are inherently engaging and enjoyable for your students;
- that require response through music, dance, or visual art;
- that simplify language through an artistic device; and
- that prompt students to consider perspectives other than their own.

Also bear in mind that there's no need to restrict a lesson or a unit to just one strategy. Multiple strategies can be woven together in imaginative ways that will excite your students based on their particular interests and aptitudes.

This Part contains three sample units illustrating how creative arts strategies can be combined at the primary, intermediate, and secondary levels. Each unit features a progression of arts-based strategies, all building toward a common goal. And each provides plenty of context in which English acquisition can occur, by making input both accessible and enjoyable for your students.

Sample Units

Primary Unit (K–3)
    Tuesday 107

Intermediate Unit (4–6)
    The Terrible Warrior 111

Secondary Unit (7–12)
    Rappaccini's Daughter 119

Primary Unit

Tuesday

Thematic Connections
- Life science
- Children's literature
- Visual arts

Materials
- Copy of the book *Tuesday*
- Paper and pen or pencil
- Hand drum
- 3D frog representation
- Post-its
- Supplies to create new wordless books
- Volume control wheel

Synopsis of *Tuesday* by David Weisner

This book is a good choice for building a unit because of the evocative nature of the pictures, the simplicity of the implied story, and the possibilities for extending it.

Tuesday is a fantasy story composed of spectacular and mysterious pictures describing how frogs invade a town. It begins in a swamp around eight o'clock on a Tuesday night, when a turtle and some fish see frogs in the air above, riding on flying lily pads.

The frogs fly en masse into town, where they engage in all kinds of mischief. After a night filled with frog shenanigans, the sun rises, the magic ends, and the frogs return to their ponds. But the townsfolk are puzzled by the lily pads they find all over the roads, and detectives begin an investigation. The story concludes when, on the following Tuesday night, pigs begin to fly into the air.

STRATEGY PROGRESSION

Infinite-Loop Motif Game — "I Give You"

Play this game with a life-like, 3D frog representation, using the line "I give you a frog."
(See page 59)

Sound Effect Stories

Using the volume control wheel, ask the children to make frog noises.
(See page 21)

Drumbeat Statues

Have students portray frogs as they play drumbeat freeze. Various rhythms can signal hopping, leaping, jumping, swimming, or sitting on a lily pad to catch flies.
(See page 71)

Sentence Stems

Ask students to fill in the following sentence stems:

Frogs can _____.
Frogs cannot _____.

Tell the students that soon they will discover whether they are correct, adding, with a dramatic flourish, that they may be quite surprised.
(See page 43)

Wordless Books

Use the wordless book *Tuesday* to elicit stories from students. Transcribe their narratives on Post-its applied to each page.
(See page 23)

Storytelling with Pantomime

While you read the story from the Post-its, have the children pantomime each role in unison.
(See page 22)

Teacher-Adapted Songs

Ask students to perform teacher-invented motions to accompany a recording of "Five Little Frogs" as sung by Raffi:

Five green speckled frogs
Sat on a speckled log
Eating some most delicious bugs (Yum, yum)
One jumped into the pool
Where it was nice and cool
Then there were four green speckled frogs

Then introduce a change in the original lyrics to:

Many green and speckled frogs
Are sitting on some speckled logs
Eating some delicious bugs (Yum, yum)
They jump up in the air
They float on lily pads way up there
Now the town is full of flying frogs

Have students sing "Five Little Frogs" with new hand motions and the adapted lyrics.
(See page 60)

Poetry: Terquain

Ask students to write a structured poem about normal frogs, using the format of a terquain. For example:

Frog
Hopping, jumping, croaking
Silly

Write the terquains on Post-its and place them on a piece of poster board at a prominent location in the room.

Next have the students write structured poems about the frogs in *Tuesday*. For example:

Frog
Floating, flying, gliding
Magical

Write the terquains on Post-its and put them on a separate piece of poster board, placed next to the first.
(See page 52)

Book Arts

Lead a brief discussion about the final page of *Tuesday*, which illustrates pigs flying above the town. Invite the children to write a wordless book, entitled *Next Tuesday*, about what happens the following week. The student authors and illustrators should be noted on the cover.

This book may be created individually or in small cooperative groups and put on display in the classroom library alongside copies of *Tuesday*.

Further activities might include creating simple text for *Next Tuesday* or introducing another structured poetic form for writing about pigs. Perhaps a different animal could take flight each Tuesday evening, producing a limitless supply of stories in your classroom. Or the unit could be used as a lead-in to other stories about frogs or as a thematic complement to the study of the life cycle of a frog.
(See page 99)

Intermediate Unit

The Terrible Warrior

Thematic Connections
- Social studies (folklore, Maasai lifestyle and culture)

Materials
- Narrative of "The Terrible Warrior" *(see pages 116–118)* and illustrations (optional)
- Volume control wheel
- Hand drum
- Supplies to create a classroom transformation and a dramatic performance
- Essential oil blend (optional)
- Hyena headbands (optional)

Synopsis of "The Terrible Warrior"

This Maasai folktale is a good choice to dramatize because the smallest creatures (analogous to children) are the cleverest. English learners will benefit from the repetitive story line and repeated refrains.

A rabbit leaves his home — a hole in the ground — and a caterpillar slithers down to take a nap. When the rabbit returns, he notices tracks outside his home and calls down, "Who is in my house?" The frightened caterpillar responds, "This is the Warrior Chief of the Neverwoz. I trample the rhinoceros underfoot, and I crush the body of the elephant!"

The rabbit, not stopping to consider the improbability of these claims, is terrified. He searches out the jackal, the leopard, the rhinoceros, and the elephant, in that order, to help him regain entry to his home. But the caterpillar scares them all away with his fierce voice.

Finally, when the rabbit has lost all hope, a little frog comes hopping along. Recognizing the absurdity of the situation, she enters the rabbit's hole, discovers the caterpillar, and presents him to the rabbit. The frog then congratulates the caterpillar on the fine joke he has played on the jackal, the leopard, the rhinoceros, and the elephant. When word gets out, all the animals have a good laugh, especially the hyenas.

112 ENGAGE

STRATEGY PROGRESSION

Sound Effect Stories

Using the volume control wheel, ask the children to make the noises of the animals that will appear in "The Terrible Warrior" — rabbits, caterpillars, frogs, jackals, leopards, rhinoceroses, elephants, and hyenas.
(See page 21)

Drumbeat Statues

Have students portray the animals that will appear in "The Terrible Warrior" — rabbits, caterpillars, frogs, jackals, leopards, rhinoceroses, elephants, and hyenas — as you play drumbeat freeze. Various rhythms can signal crawling, hopping, leaping, jumping, crouching, and running in fear.
(See page 71)

Storytelling with Pantomime

Give a dramatic reading of "The Terrible Warrior" *(see pages 116–118)* while displaying pictures of the animals featured in the story. Reread the story, asking all of the children to pantomime all of the parts simultaneously. If appropriate, read the story for a third time, with the children choosing the parts they would like to pantomime.
(See page 22)

Sound Effect Stories

Using the volume control wheel, have students practice the caterpillar's refrain at different vocal intensities:

This is the Warrior Chief of the Neverwoz. I trample the rhinoceros underfoot, and dance upon the body of the elephant!
(See page 21)

Folktale Dramatizations

Dramatize "The Terrible Warrior" through sequential, scaffolded steps, making sure to include all students in the final performance. This can be accomplished by using character groups rather than individual roles. For example, instead of one elephant, cast several elephants.

The gender of the animals can be changed to accommodate the actors. For example, the elephant can be female and the frog can be male.

If students have difficulty with the transitions from scene to scene, the teacher can take the role of the narrator to verbally move the story along. The dialogue, however, should always be performed by the students.
(See page 26)

Classroom Transformation

Present the dramatized folktale to parents or to other classes in the school. Begin by creating an evocative atmosphere for the performance. Engage students in researching the arid landscape of Maasai territory in East Africa. Then redesign the classroom to fit the setting of the story.

When designing the space, make sure there is ample room for an audience, for example, in a clearing in the grassland. Headbands with hyena ears can be constructed and given to audience members, who will be asked to provide a chorus of laughter at the end of the story.
(See page 85)

Aromas to Evoke Mood

Use the following blend of essential oils to replicate the aroma of the arid grasslands in which the folktale takes place:

Ingredients

Sage	10 drops
Frankincense	25 drops
Atlas Cedarwood	40 drops
Water	4 ounces

Directions

Fill a glass or plastic spray container with one ounce of water. Add the drops of Sage, Frankincense, and Atlas Cedarwood and shake the mixture gently. Add the rest of the water and shake again. Spray as needed. The fragrance will remain in the air for about 15 minutes.

This blend creates a warm, spicy aroma with warming yet relaxing properties *(for more on aromatherapy, see pages 39–40)*.

Extension

The recipe above is composed of oils commonly sold in North America. However, if available, the following African essential oils can add authenticity:

- African Wild Sage-Leleshwa
- African Frankincense-Opponax
- Yohimbe Bark Extract
- Myrrh
- Pygeum
- Kola Nut

Jazz Chants

Create jazz chants about "The Terrible Warrior" that can be incorporated into the performance. For example, the following words can be chanted by the rabbit every time he seeks help from another animal:

Jackal, jackal, please help me,
A monster's in my house, come and see.

Change the word "jackal" to "leopard," to "rhinoceros," and finally to "elephant" at the appropriate times.

The chant below can be repeated by the jackal, the leopard, the rhinoceros, the elephant, and the frog, in succession.

Who is in Rabbit's house?
You better hurry and get out!

When performing for another group of children, the audience can participate by joining in on the chant.
(See page 66)

Performance of "The Terrible Warrior"

Make a program booklet for the dramatization. You may want to include information about the Maasai people, past and the present, as well as short biographies of the cast.

Have students design and create costumes as needed. These may range from the symbolic to the elaborate, depending on classroom resources and student interest. Sometimes skilled parents enjoy making costumes for their own children as well as for others.

Decide on a date for the performance in your classroom and invite a succession of other classrooms to attend. Let parents, administrators, and other educators attend at the time of their choice.

"The Terrible Warrior"

A Maasai Folktale from East Africa
Adapted and Retold for English Language Learners
by Sharon Adelman Reyes

Once upon a time, a rabbit left his home, a cozy little hole in the ground, to look for food. While the rabbit was away, a caterpillar crawled inside his house and took a nap. When the rabbit returned home, he noticed new footprints on the ground going into the hole and he called out, "Who is in my house?"

The caterpillar was frightened. He knew the rabbit was much bigger than he was. So he tried to scare the rabbit away. The caterpillar cried out in his loudest voice, "This is the Warrior Chief of the Neverwoz. I trample the rhinoceros underfoot, and I crush the body of the elephant!"

Now the rabbit was frightened. He imagined that a huge monster had squeezed into his home. If this terrible warrior could trample the rhinoceros and crush the elephant, he could easily destroy a rabbit! So the rabbit quickly hopped away to find help.

Soon the rabbit met a jackal. He said, "Jackal, Jackal, please help me. There is a terrible warrior in my house and he will not leave. Can you make him go away so I can go home?"

The jackal agreed to help, and he went back with the rabbit. When they were outside of the rabbit's house, the jackal called down into the hole in a loud voice, "Who is in my friend Rabbit's home? Come out at once!"

Inside the hole, the caterpillar was nervous, but he still tried to sound fierce. He called out, "This is the Warrior Chief of the Neverwoz. I trample the rhinoceros underfoot, and I crush the body of the elephant!"

The jackal trembled in fear. He did not want to be crushed or trampled. And so, the jackal slunk off in shame.

The rabbit hopped off to get help, this time from the leopard. When he found the leopard, he said "Leopard, Leopard, please help me. There is a terrible warrior in my house and he will not leave. Can you make him go away so I can go home?"

The leopard agreed, and went back with the rabbit. When they were outside the rabbit's house, the leopard roared down into the hole, "Who is in my friend Rabbit's home? Come out at once or I will eat you up!"

Inside the hole, the caterpillar was more frightened than ever, but he called out even more fiercely, "This is the Warrior Chief of the Neverwoz. I trample the rhinoceros underfoot, and I crush the body of the elephant!"

The leopard shook in terror. He did not want to be crushed or trampled upon, so he ran off as fast as he could.

The poor rabbit was losing hope of ever going home again, but he did not give up. "I had better look for the rhinoceros and the elephant," he thought, "for they must certainly be more fierce that this terrible warrior."

When the rabbit found the rhinoceros, he said "Rhinoceros, Rhinoceros, please help me. There is a terrible warrior in my house and he will not leave. Can you make him go away so I can go home?"

The rhinoceros was a proud creature. "Don't worry," he said. "No other creature on this earth is fiercer than me. I will frighten this so-called terrible warrior right out of your house!" He went back with the rabbit. When they were outside the rabbit's house, the rhinoceros bellowed down into the hole, "Who is in my friend Rabbit's home? Come out at once or I will smash you with one foot."

Inside the hole, the caterpillar shook with terror, but he called out more fiercely than he ever had before in his life, "This is the Warrior Chief of the Neverwoz. I trample the rhinoceros underfoot, and I crush the body of the elephant!"

"Trample me!" exclaimed the rhinoceros. "That could cause wrinkles. I have enough wrinkles already. I surely do not need any more!" The truth was that the rhinoceros was just as frightened as the jackal and the leopard, but he did not want to admit that to the rabbit. He had to protect his reputation as a ferocious beast! So the rhinoceros went crashing off back to his home.

The rabbit had only one choice left. He went off to find the elephant. When the rabbit found the elephant he said "Elephant, Elephant, please help me. There is a terrible warrior in my house and he will not leave. Not even the rhinoceros can make him leave. Can you make him go away so I can go home?"

The elephant was not one to be outdone by the rhinoceros! "Don't worry," he said. "I can do what the rhinoceros could not do. I will frighten this so-called terrible warrior right out of your house!"

The elephant went back with the rabbit. When they were outside the rabbit's house, the elephant trumpeted down into the hole, "Who is in my friend Rabbit's home? Come out at once or I will send my trunk down into the hole, I will scoop you out, and I will make a quick end of you."

Inside the hole, the caterpillar shivered with terror, but he had no other choice than to make his voice boom like thunder, "This is the Warrior Chief of the Neverwoz. I trample the rhinoceros underfoot, and I crush the body of the elephant!"

The caterpillar's voice was so loud that the ground shook. The elephant thought, "If I put my trunk down into that hole, I might not ever be able to get it back out!" But the elephant could not admit that he was as cowardly as the rhinoceros, so he told the rabbit, "Oh no, I forgot I have to go to the water hole before dinner." Then he lumbered away.

Poor Rabbit! He did not know what else to do, so he sat outside on the ground near his hole and cried.

A little frog came hopping by. "What is wrong? Why are you crying?" asked the little frog.

The rabbit replied through his tears, "The Warrior Chief of the Neverwoz is in my house and will not come out. He can trample the rhinoceros underfoot and crush the body of the elephant, and so no animal can help me!"

"How do you know this trespasser is so terrible?" asked the frog.

"Because he says so," sobbed the rabbit.

"Well, then, we must find out if he is telling the truth," declared the frog.

The frog called down into the hole, "Who is in my friend Rabbit's home? Come out at once so I can see you."

"This is the Warrior Chief of the Neverwoz. I trample the rhinoceros underfoot, and I crush the body of the elephant," shouted the caterpillar.

The frog was not frightened in the least. She knew that such a fierce creature could never fit inside of a rabbit's hole. So she hopped down and looked around. There, on the ground, was a tiny little caterpillar.

The frog croaked with laughter.

"Please don't hurt me!" cried the caterpillar.

"Don't worry," replied the frog. "You have played a fine joke on all of our cowardly friends who did not think before they ran away. You should be congratulated. Please come with me, so we can show Rabbit who this terrible warrior is!"

Together the frog and the caterpillar went out to see the rabbit. When the rabbit saw who had made him so afraid, he felt very foolish, but not nearly as foolish as the jackal, the leopard, the rhinoceros, and the elephant.

When the story got out that they had been frightened by a caterpillar with a loud voice, all of the other animals laughed and laughed. The hyenas are still laughing.

SECONDARY UNIT

Rappaccini's Daughter

Thematic Connections
- History
- Literature
- Science
- Ethics

Materials
- Readers Theater scripts *(see Resource on page 128)*
- Symbolic props and costumes
- Copies of "Rappaccini's Rap" *(see pages 125–126)*
- Calligraphy tools
- Index cards
- Supplies to create artists' books, program booklets, mind maps, and self-portraits
- Audio equipment (optional)
- Essential oil spray (optional)
- PowerPoint background slides (optional)
- Video equipment (optional)

SYNOPSIS OF "RAPPACCINI'S DAUGHTER" BY NATHANIEL HAWTHORNE

The two central characters in this story are romantically involved and simultaneously caught up in an unusual moral dilemma. This makes "Rappaccini's Daughter" an ideal choice for secondary school students, who can usually identify with both of these predicaments. The narrative from which Hawthorne's story is probably drawn can be traced back to a traditional folktale from India.

Giacomo Rappaccini, a medical researcher in medieval Padua, Italy, cultivates a garden of poisonous plants. Rappaccini brings up his daughter, Beatrice, to tend the plants. In the process, Beatrice becomes resistant to the poisons herself, but poisonous to others.

A young man, Giovanni Guasconti, moves to Padua to attend the university there. He obtains a room overlooking Rappaccini's lush, locked garden. From this vantage point, Giovanni is able to view the lovely Beatrice, who is confined within, as she tends her father's plants. After gaining entrance to the garden through a housekeeper who has a key to the locked gate, he meets and falls in love with the mysterious Beatrice.

Giovanni eventually notices Beatrice's troubling effect on the plants in the garden. He sees fresh flowers wither and insects die when exposed to her breath. Giovanni's mentor, Professor Pietro Baglioni, warns him that Rappaccini is not to be trusted. But, having fallen in love with Beatrice, Giovanni ignores his advice.

Soon Giovanni begins to notice the consequences of his association with Beatrice. He must admit that she is poisonous and that he is becoming poisonous as well. In the meantime, Baglioni gives Giovanni a small vial, explaining that it contains the antidote for Beatrice's poison.

Giovanni confronts Beatrice with his new knowledge of her nature. She urges him to look past her poisonous exterior to see her pure and innocent essence. Giovanni produces the vial filled with the antidote, believing that by sharing it with Beatrice they will be able to stay together. She grabs the vial in order to check its safety by drinking it first. But the only antidote for her poison is death, and Beatrice dies in the garden as Rappaccini looks on.

STRATEGY PROGRESSION

Opening Question

Ask students the following question and discuss their answers:
What would you do if you fell in love and then discovered the person you had fallen in love with was actually poisonous?

Explain that this dilemma was the basis for a short story by Nathaniel Hawthorne. Then provide background about the author and his times *(see www.hawthorneinsalem.org)*, which will flow naturally into the Readers Theater script.

Readers Theater

Choose a script for "Rappaccini's Daughter" *(see page 128 for a source)*. Hand it out to your students and give them time to read silently. Or send the scripts home to be read before class. Discuss the story, then ask for volunteers for the specific roles.

Arrange chairs in a semicircle at the front of the room. Seat the characters in accordance with their relationships and interactions with each other.

Distribute symbolic props and costume pieces. Do multiple readings of the script, rotating characters to ensure everyone has a chance to participate.

Turn the classroom into a theater and stage multiple productions so that roles can be filled by various students.

Students who choose not to play characters can assist in other ways, such as ushering, creating props and costumes, or overseeing technical aspects of the production.

Make a program booklet for the performance. You may want to include historical information about the original story and its author, as well as short biographies of the cast and crew.

Evoke an aura of mystery though the use of music. Use backdrops with projected PowerPoint images that the students have researched. Dim the lights between scenes.
(See page 32)

Before the beginning of scenes that incorporate the scent of poisonous flowers, spray a sweet floral essential oil in the air while the lights are off.
(see the recipe on page 122)

Invite other classrooms to attend. The production can scaffold literature for all students in your school — Hawthorne can be difficult! — while creating an enjoyable performance for all audience members.

Research the traditional Indian folktale that inspired Hawthorne.

View the film *Rappaccini's Daughter*
(see www.imdb.com/title/tt0081403/). Contrast the film to the original literature and to the Readers Theater script. Critique the film.

Aromas to Evoke Mood

Use the following blend of essential oils to create a sweet, exotic aroma that evokes the flower garden where Beatrice is confined:

Ingredients

Lavender	30 drops
Sweet Orange	42 drops
Geranium	7 drops
Water	4 ounces

Directions

Fill a glass or plastic spray container with one ounce of water. Add the drops of Lavender, Sweet Orange, and Geranium and shake the mixture gently. Add the rest of the water and shake again. Spray as needed. The fragrance will remain in the air for about 15 minutes *(for more on aromatherapy, see pages 39–40).*

Readers Theater Performance Suggestion

Spray the essential oil blend into the air between the appropriate scenes while the lights are dimmed. Vary the amount of spray used as the performance reaches its conclusion. Begin with a subtle aroma and end with an intense sweetness.

Greek Chorus

Discuss critical issues brought forward by the story, such as What is ethical in the name of scientific research? and Do ends justify means? Explore these and other salient themes though the use of a Greek chorus *(see pages 36–38).* Let the students compose and add the lines of the Greek chorus to the Readers Theater script.

Structured Poetry

Create structured poems on the theme of "Rappaccini's Daughter" or from the perspective of one of the characters in the story *(for more on structured poetry, see page 52)*. For example:

Haiku
Flowers are growing
Lovely purple fragrant blooms
Do not believe them

Tanka
Flowers are growing
Lovely purple fragrant blooms
Do not believe them
They beckon, they entice you
If you follow you are doomed

Terquain
Love
Falling, soaring, collapsing
Confusion

Cinquain
Daughter
Kind, captive
Imprisoned, sequestered, caged
Sadness, melancholy, grief, longing
Beatrice

Diamante
Antidote
warm, bright
smile, laugh, dance
remedy, cure, venom, toxicant
shiver, tremble, crush
cold, still
poison

Calligraphy

Write the poems on unlined index cards using calligraphy.
(See page 92)

Mind Maps

Create a mind map from the perspective of one of the characters in "Rappaccini's Daughter," for example, about Giovanni's conflicting views of Beatrice or about Beatrice's thought process regarding her father.
(See page 90)

Self-Portrait

In an extension of the original activity, draw a "self-portrait" that one of the characters might have created of himself or herself.
(See page 93)

Book Arts

Create an interpretive book about the story using structured poetry, mind maps, and self-portraits. Divide the students into cooperative groups and ask them to produce one artist's book per group. The groups can be offered choices in book types or they can all make the same variety.
(See page 99)

Rap

In cooperative groups, read "Rappaccini's Rap" below. Each group discusses the meaning of these original lyrics, then looks for metaphor and the following rhyme types:

- Perfect rhyme
- Multisyllabic rhyme
- Internal rhyme
- Slant rhyme
- Identical rhyme
- Rich rhyme
- Assonant rhyme
- Consonant rhyme
- Macaronic rhyme

(See pages 47–51)

RAPPACCINI'S RAP
By Sharon Adelman Reyes

I've got some lovely plants, young man, I've got Beatrice, my daughter
Come down into my garden and for Beatrice you'll be water
Give her a kiss, when you leave you will miss her mysterious charm
I have raised her with love, don't worry, what's the harm? *[Repeat]*

I want Beatrice to marry — how far should a dad go?
If I see you breathe her essence, should I stop and tell you "No"?
I won't tell you whoa, won't let you go, won't ever say no, because I know
It's what I planned all these years, how easily, how eagerly you are lured
If I see you touch her gently, if I see you grip her hand
I will hide and slyly chuckle, "Now forever you're her man!"
So I'll lure you to my garden, let the housemaid have the key
I will tell her to entice you, that soon Beatrice you will see
No matter what they say, Beatrice will pull you back
They will tell you, "Go home, just say no, just turn your back."

But it's mysterious, so mysterious, makes you delirious, so delirious
It is la-la-la-la-la-la-love, you are filled, so filled
It is la-la-la-la-la-la-love, so you fold, you fold
This is real, real, real, real, it is no prank
From love you reel, reel, reel, reel, you are a man
You may try to escape, but you can't, no you can't

I've got some lovely plants, young man, I've got Beatrice, my daughter
Come down into my garden and for Beatrice you'll be water
Give her a kiss, when you leave you will miss her mysterious charm
I have raised her with love, don't worry, what's the harm? *[Repeat]*

You have come into my garden, which for me is no surprise
When you look into her eyes, my Beatrice tells no lies
I surmise that you have found that you cannot leave, but do not grieve
For you have what all men crave, you have power and men will fear you
So enjoy this tender moment, do not fight it, hold her near you
Wait! Stop! Whoa! No! Don't drink what's in that vial!
Wait! Stop! Whoa! No! Don't drink it, for its vile! It is vile!
She drank it, she is falling, she is sinking to the ground
Oh my daughter, you are my water, without you I am lost
I never once imagined love for science would have such cost
Goodbye my princess, goodbye my angel, fragrant child, ciao bella,
Oh, Giovanni, we are united in our grieving, I now tell ya
Sister flower my dear daughter, fragrant purple, silent hurtful
Lost your sister, lost my daughter, gained a son who's not compliant
So welcome to my garden, it's now yours as it was hers, catch
A bride through garden windows and I'll have grandchildren of science

I've got some lovely plants, young man, I've got Beatrice, my daughter
Come down into my garden and for Beatrice you'll be water
Give her a kiss, when you leave you will miss her mysterious charm
I have raised her with love, don't worry, what's the harm? *[Repeat]*

Each group composes an original rap based on the story of "Rappaccini's Daughter," rehearses it, and creates a video in which it is featured. The class views all the rap videos they have created.

Part IV
Resources

Second Language Acquisition

Stephen D. Krashen. *The Input Hypothesis: Issues and Implications.* London and New York: Longman, 1985.

> A comprehensive overview of Krashen's theory of how language is acquired, along with responses to critics and suggestions for application, including a detailed explanation of sheltered subject matter instruction.

Stephen D. Krashen. *Explorations in Language Acquisition and Use.* Portsmouth, NH: Heinemann, 2003.

> Reviews the research showing the limits of direct instruction in language, the positive effects of free voluntary reading, and how reading and writing impact cognitive development.

Stephen D. Krashen and Tracy D. Terrell. *The Natural Approach: Language Acquisition in the Classroom.* Hayward, CA: Alemany Press, 1983.

> A practical application of Krashen's Input Hypothesis to teaching ESL to beginning English learners.

James J. Asher. *Learning Another Language Through Actions,* 7th ed. Los Gatos, CA: Sky Oak Productions, 2012.

> A step-by step guide to the Total Physical Response methodology of ESL.

Constructivism

Beverly Falk. *Teaching the Way Children Learn.* New York: Teachers College Press, 2009.

> A highly readable guide to constructivist practices, stressing the importance of active learning and "teaching for understanding." Falk also provides useful historical and theoretical context about child-centered education.

Sharon Adelman Reyes and James Crawford. *Diary of a Bilingual School: How a Constructivist Curriculum, a Multicultural Perspective, and a Commitment to Dual Immersion Education Combined to Foster Fluent Bilingualism in Spanish- and English-Speaking Children.* Portland, OR: DiversityLearningK12, 2012.

> Tracing a year in the life of a 2nd grade bilingual classroom, this book features narratives describing a curriculum based on discovery and its impact on children, along with analysis of how it worked.

Dramatic Arts

Viola Spolin. *Improvisation for the Theatre: A Handbook of Teaching and Directing Techniques.* Evanston, IL: Northwestern University Press, 1999.

> A classic that has influenced the fields of education, mental health, social work, and psychology. Although it is not specifically geared toward language acquisition, the book includes many activities that can be adapted by creative educators.

Viola Spolin. *Theatre Games for the Classroom: A Teacher's Handbook.* Evanston, IL: Northwestern University Press, 1986.

> Includes improvisational techniques and games that are designed specifically for classroom use. Their purpose is to increase self-awareness while teaching the basic elements of storytelling, literary criticism, and character analysis.

Readers Theater

Suzanne I. Barchers and Jennifer L. Kroll. *Classic Readers Theatre for Young Adults.* Greenwood Village, CO: Teachers Ideas Press, 2002.

> U.S. copyright law now protects literary rights for the life of the author plus 70 years. Thus commercially published scripts for Readers Theater — like those featured by Barchers and Kroll — are usually adapted from classic literature in the public domain. This volume is an excellent source of scripts adapted from fiction (including "Rappaccini's Daughter"), along with stage production ideas.

> Copyright restrictions generally do not prevent teachers from using or adapting short excerpts from contemporary literature for educational, noncommercial purposes (legally described as "fair use") in their classrooms. When in doubt, however, simply write to the publisher and ask permission.

Aromas to Evoke Mood

Kathi Keville and Mindy Green. *Aroma Therapy: A Complete Guide to the Healing Art.* Berkeley, CA: Crossing Press, 2009.

> A comprehensive introduction to aromatherapy, including a list of essential oils that are commonly available, along with techniques for blending and using them.

Greek Chorus

An excellent overview of Greek theater and the role of the Greek chorus by N.S. Gill can be found at: ancienthistory.about.com/od/greekliterature/a/GreekTheater.htm.

Poetry for Choral Reading

The Collected Poems of Langston Hughes, edited by Arnold Rampersad and David Roessel. New York: Vintage, 1994.

> A poetry collection that's especially suited to choral adaptation because of its accessible language and focus on everyday life. Many of Hughes's poems explore themes of social justice, such as "Let America Be America Again" (excerpted and adapted on page 31), which should interest and challenge older students.

Children's Poetry Anthologies

The Poetry Foundation offers an extensive list of poetry anthologies for children at: www.poetryfoundation.org/children/essential/ant. Here is a sampling:

Arnold Adoff, ed. *My Black Me: A Beginning Book of Black Poetry.* New York: Dutton, 1994.

Barbara Brenner. *The Earth Is Painted Green: A Garden of Poems about Our Planet.* New York: Scholastic, 1994.

Lori Marie Carlson. *Cool Salsa: Bilingual Poems on Growing Up Latino in the United States.* New York: Henry Holt, 1994.

Margaret Ferguson, Mary Jo Salter, and Jon Stallworthy, eds. *The Norton Anthology of Poetry,* 5th ed. New York: W.W. Norton, 2004.

Lee Bennett Hopkins. *Days to Celebrate: A Full Year of Poetry, People, Holidays, History, Fascinating Facts, and More.* New York: HarperCollins, 2005.

Wade Hudson, ed. *Pass It On: African American Poetry for Children.* New York: Scholastic, 1993.

Bruce Lansky, ed. *A Bad Case of the Giggles: Kids' Favorite Funny Poems.* Deephaven, MN: Meadowbrook Press, 1994.

Naomi Shihab Nye. *This Same Sky: A Collection of Poems from Around the World.* New York: Four Winds Press, 1992.

Jack Prelutsky. *The Beauty of the Beast: Poems from the Animal Kingdom.* New York: Knopf, 1997.

Jane Yolen. *Sky Scrape, City Scape: Poems of City Life.* Honesdale, PA: Boyds Mills, 1996.

Storytelling with Immigrants and Refugees

English learners who are recent immigrants and refugees often pose challenges when educators are unprepared for them. Barbara Nykiel-Herbert provides creative ideas for meeting their needs through oral and written storytelling. Here are two examples:

"Iraqi Refugee Students: From a Collection of Refugees to a Community of Learners." *Multicultural Education* 17, no. 3 (Spring 2010): 2–14. Available at: diversitylearningk12.com/articles/Nykiel-Herbert_From_a_Collection_of_Refugees.pdf.

"Constructivist Classroom Connections: Intermediate Newcomers Meet the Universal Chicken," including "Guidelines for Practice." In Sharon Adelman Reyes and Trina Lynn Vallone, *Constructivist Strategies for Teaching English Language Learners.* Thousand Oaks, CA: Corwin Press, 2008.

Children's Games from Around the World

Many games incorporate elements of the creative arts and can be easily adapted for English learners. Besides offering a source of comprehensible input, they can provide a multicultural context for classroom activities. Games appropriate for second language students are widely available on the Internet; two recommended websites are highlighted here:

Topics: Online Magazine for Learners of English provides an extensive listing of traditional games from countries including Venezuela, Mexico, Korea, China, and Germany: www.topics-mag.com/edition11/games-section.htm.

The Tulsa Global Alliance, a nonprofit, volunteer organization, features a "Kids' World International Curriculum," much of which is adapted from *Games of the World: How to Make Them, How to Play Them, How They Came to Be,* by Frederic V. Grunfeld, published by the Swiss Committee for UNICEF in 1982: webpages.shepherd.edu/EMORRI01/KWCurriculum_Games.pdf.

Narrated Children's Symphonies

Many symphonic renditions of music for children are readily available. If you are not sure where to begin, you can't go wrong by selecting performances by Leonard Bernstein, such as those highlighted in this book:

Bernstein Favorites: Children's Classics (1991), including *Peter and the Wolf,* by Sergei Prokofiev; *Carnival of the Animals,* by Camille Saint-Saëns; and *The Young Person's Guide to the Orchestra,* by Benjamin Britten.

The Sorcerer's Apprentice by Paul Dukas, performed by the New York Philharmonic, conducted by Leonard Bernstein and narrated by Marshall Izen (2008).

Play Party Songs and Games

Cheryl Warren Mattox. *Shake It to the One That you Love the Best: Play Songs and Lullabies from Black Musical Traditions.* Nashville, TN: JTG of Nashville, 1990.

A highly recommended collection of play party songs, games, and lullabies. It includes beautiful illustrations from the works of Varnette P. Honeywood and Brenda Joysmith, along with an accompanying musical track.

World Music

Many fine sources of world music are easily available. Here are two that encompass a wide variety of cultures and countries.

The Rough Guides to World Music can be found at: www.worldmusic.net. They highlight music from Africa, Europe, and the Middle East (vol. 1), Latin and North America, the Caribbean, India, Asia, and the Pacific (vol. 2).

Putumayo World Music is another online source of quality world music recordings, which can be found at: www.putumayo.com.

Jazz Chants

Catherine Graham. *Jazz Chants.* New York: Oxford University Press, 1978.

Compiled by a pioneer in the adaption of Jazz Chants for teaching English as a second language. To order Graham's books, audio CDs, and audiobooks, visit her website at: jazzchants.net/who-is-carolyn-graham.

Songs and Poems for Dance and Movement

Many songs recorded by the children's musical artist Raffi make excellent choices for dramatization and dance. The following songs, highlighted in this book, are available through Rounder Records at: www.rounder.com.

"In My Garden" in *One Light, One Sun* (1985) and "Let's Make Some Noise" in *Everything Grows* (1996).

The poem excerpted for use with creative movement activities can be found in:

Nancy White Carlstrom. *Wild Wild Sunflower Child Anna.* New York: Scholastic, 1987.

Dance Websites

Video clips of professional dance concerts are available at the following websites.

Alvin Ailey American Dance Theatre: www.alvinailey.org.
Appalachian Spring: www.youtube.com/watch?v=E1o65tCZTWA.
Pilobolus Dance Theatre: www.pilobolus.com.

Origami

OrigamiUSA is a not-for-profit, tax-exempt, educational and cultural arts organization dedicated to the sharing of paper-folding in America and around the world. It has a mail-order supply center, The Origami Source, which sells origami books, papers, and videos.

OrigamiUSA can be accessed at: www.origamiusa.org.

Book Arts

Here are some titles that contain creative ideas and instructions on book-making.

Linda Fry Kenzle. *Pages: Innovative Bookmaking Techniques.* Iola, WI: Krause Publications, 1998.

Alisa Golden. *Making Handmade Books: 100 + Bindings, Structures & Forms.* New York: Lark Crafts, 2011.

Heather Weston. *Bookcraft: Techniques for Binding, Folding, and Decorating to Create Books and More.* Beverly, MA: Quarry Books, 2008.

Calligraphy

Don Marsh. *Calligraphy.* Cincinnati, OH: North Light Books, 1996.

Among the many books available on calligraphy, this one is an excellent way to get beginners started.

Free Reading

Stephen D. Krashen. *Free Voluntary Reading.* Santa Barbara: Libraries Unlimited, 2011.

Stephen D. Krashen. *The Power of Reading: Insights from the Research,* 2nd ed. Westport, CT and Portsmouth, NH: Libraries Unlimited and Heinemann, 2004.

For those seeking research evidence on the benefits of free voluntary reading, these books are an excellent place to start. Highly recommended.

Donalyn Miller. *The Book Whisperer: Awakening the Inner Reader in Every Child.* San Francisco: Jossey-Bass, 2009.

A book that's full of ideas for encouraging free voluntary reading with your students.

Fine Arts in Spanish

Sharon Adelman Reyes, Salvador Gabaldón, and José Severo Morejón. *La Palabra Justa: A Glossary for K–12 Bilingual Teachers.* Portland, OR: DiversityLearningK12 (in press).

A Spanish-English/English-Spanish glossary featuring terms from academic content areas, technology, and school life, along with extensive coverage of the visual and performing arts.

Glossary

Educational Philosophy

A philosophy of knowledge and how it is acquired — in other words, a theory of how "knowing" takes place — and what that implies for teaching.

Constructivism

An educational philosophy that conceives learning as an active process of reconciling prior understandings with new information and experiences, causing us to build and rebuild concepts to make sense of the world as we discover it.

Behaviorism

An educational philosophy that conceives learning as an externally directed process of instilling desired behaviors through repetition and reinforcement, stressing teacher-centered models of "delivering" instruction.

Methodology

A way of applying an educational philosophy to teaching.

Strategy

A way of applying a methodology to teaching through a planned learning activity that uses appropriate techniques and aims toward a specific pedagogical goal.

Techniques

Common, everyday practices that flow from a methodology and become second nature to experienced teachers.

Framework

A basic conceptual structure, encompassing methodologies, strategies, and techniques to guide teaching and learning.

Sheltering

A methodology to foster second language acquisition that uses linguistic, visual, or contextual techniques to make input comprehensible.

Scaffolding

A methodology in which various temporary supports are provided to learners to enable them to perform at higher levels than they could on their own.

Language Acquisition

A subconscious process in which language is mastered incidentally, effortlessly, and without conscious study.

Language Learning

A conscious process of learning the formal aspects of language, such as rules of grammar, usage, and vocabulary.

Comprehensible Input

Understandable messages through which languages are acquired.

Output

Use of language through speech or writing; the result, not the cause, of language acquisition.

Affective filter

One or more psychological barriers that keep comprehensible input from getting through, blocking the process of language acquisition.

Acknowledgments

THIS BOOK WOULD NOT EXIST without the work of Stephen Krashen. His theory of second language acquisition — along with its practical application through the concept of sheltered instruction — has revolutionized the fields of bilingual and ESL education. It also provides a foundation for the ENGAGE Framework and for many of the strategies featured here. I am greatly indebted to Steve, both for helping to refine my thinking on directions this book might take and for offering thoughtful commentary on the final draft.

Several other colleagues generously agreed to review the manuscript as well. For their insightful suggestions, I wish to thank Brigid Burke, Assistant Professor of Education and World Language Education Program Coordinator at Bowling Green State University (OH); Mary Carol Combs, Professor of Practice, Department of Teaching, Learning and Sociocultural Studies, University of Arizona; Cynthia Cosgrave, a former ESOL/Bilingual Instructor at Lewis & Clark College in Portland, OR; Michelle Gambardella, Education Specialist at Carpentersville School District (IL); and Trina Vallone, Associate Professor of Education at Trinity Christian College in Palos Heights, IL.

Some of the strategies highlighted in this book are my original creations, developed over the course of my nearly four decades in education. Others are adapted from widely known practices in teaching. For the remainder, I would like to acknowledge assistance from the following:

> Mary Carol Combs contributed the Greek Chorus strategy on pages 36–38.
>
> Melissa Ketrenos provided expert consultation on the Aromas to Evoke Mood strategy on page 39 and contributed the two aroma recipes used in Part III.
>
> For the Self-Portraits strategy on page 93, I took helpful ideas from *Arts Alive: Teacher's Guide*. Bloomington, IN: Agency for Instructional Television, 1984.

Trina Vallone contributed the Multimedia Essay strategy and Technology Tips on pages 96–97.

I am also grateful for permission to reprint the following graphic material:

Cover painting and reproduction on page 95: Copyright © 2013 by Melissa Ketrenos. All rights reserved.

Page 37: Woodcut of "Rappaccini's Daughter" from Nathaniel Hawthorne's *Works* (Globe Edition, 1880), courtesy of Hawthorne in Salem Website: www.hawthorneinsalem.org.

Page 91: Mind map from Herrera, Socorro G.; Murry, Kevin G.; and Cabral, Robin M. *Assessment Accommodations for Classroom Teachers of Culturally and Linguistically Diverse Students*, 2nd ed., 2013, page 114. Reprinted by permission of Pearson Education, Inc., Upper Saddle River, NJ.

Page 98: "Let Peace Blossom," by teacher/muralist Michelle Obregon and the students of Konawaena High School, Kealakekua, HI.

A final word of thanks: The ideas in this book began to take shape long ago, when I found myself contrasting my own teaching style to that of the dominant pedagogical model. But without the support of my husband, Jim Crawford, those ideas would never have evolved into this project. When I first proposed the concept, Jim enthusiastically encouraged me. But he did not stop there. He pushed my thinking on every aspect of the work from the framework to the strategies, critiqued countless drafts, and then went on to oversee production, from laying out the pages and selecting the graphics, to editing and typesetting the text, to creating the cover design. His confidence in my ability to think, to create, and to write continues to inspire my work and propel me always forward.

Be a Contributor!

Have you created a strategy you would like to share?

You are invited to help us in developing and expanding the ENGAGE Framework.

We are looking for effective sheltering and scaffolding strategies not only in the Creative Arts, but also in Language Arts, Math, Science, and Social Studies.

Please send your classroom ideas and experiences to sharon@diversitylearningk12.com.

With your permission — plus full credit, of course — we may want to use your strategy in future editions.

About DiversityLearningK12

Specializing in bilingual, ESL, and multicultural education, DiversityLearningK12 is a consulting group that provides professional development, keynote presentations, program design, educational publishing, and related services. For more information, please visit us at www.diversitylearningk12.com or email us at info@diversitylearningk12.com.

Also Available from DiversityLearningK12 ...

"A must read for parents and teachers who value bilingualism, biculturalism, and positive identity construction for their children. Highly recommended."
— *Choice*

"Refreshing and inspiring ... If you are interested in learning how educators and parents can promote language acquisition, creating inventors who think creatively and (gasp!) even achieve excellent results on academic tests, this is the book for you."
— *Creative Educator*

"The beauty of *Diary of a Bilingual School* is that anyone can read this book and gain something from it. Parents of bilingual children will learn tools on how to help their children's education thrive. Bilingual educators and administrators will gain insights and tips on how to create the best bilingual classroom experience possible."
— *Multilingual Living*

Diary of a Bilingual School

Sharon Adelman Reyes & James Crawford

2012, 136 pages, 6" x 9"
ISBN: 978-0-9847317-0-1
Paperback: $19.95; Amazon Kindle: $4.99
Bulk orders: info@diversitylearningk12.com

DUAL IMMERSION, a popular new way to cultivate bilingualism, is capturing the attention of parents and educators alike. By bringing together children from diverse backgrounds to learn each other's languages in a natural setting, it has proved far more effective at cultivating fluency than traditional approaches.

But how do these programs actually work? What goes on in dual immersion classrooms? And what is it that makes them so effective?

Diary of a Bilingual School answers these questions with a unique mix of narratives and analysis. Depicting a year in the life of a 2nd grade classroom, it demonstrates what can happen when the instruction is bilingual and the curriculum is constructivist.

The book focuses on Chicago's Inter-American Magnet School, one of the nation's most acclaimed dual immersion programs, where children thrive in an environment that unlocks their intellectual curiosity and enthusiasm for learning. Simultaneously, without conscious effort, they become proficient in two languages and at home in a culture that differs from their own.

For those who want to discover the benefits of dual immersion for their children or for their students—or who want to learn more about child-centered approaches to teaching—*Diary of a Bilingual School* is a must.

DiversityLearningK12
P.O. BOX 19790
PORTLAND, OREGON 97280

www.ingramcontent.com/pod-product-compliance
Lightning Source LLC
Chambersburg PA
CBHW080249170426
43192CB00014BA/2619